INSIDE FORENSIC SCIENCE

Forensic Anthropology

Bradley J. Adams, Ph.D.

SERIES EDITOR | Lawrence Kobilinsky, Ph.D.

CHELSEA HOUSE
PUBLISHERS
An imprint of Infobase Publishing

Forensic Anthropology

Chelsea House
An imprint of Infobase Publishing
132 West 31st Street
New York NY 10001

Library of Congress Cataloging-in-Publication Data

Adams, Bradley J.
  Forensic anthropology / Bradley J. Adams.
      p. cm. — (Inside forensic science)
  Includes bibliographical references and index.
  ISBN 0-7910-9198-8 (hardcover)
  1. Forensic anthropology—Juvenile literature. I. Title. II. Series.
  GN69.8.A33 2006
  614'.17—dc22   2006011030

Chelsea House books are available at special discounts when purchased in bulk
quantities for businesses, associations, institutions, or sales promotions. Please call
our Special Sales Department in New York at (212) 967-8800 or (800) 322-8755.

You can find Chelsea House on the World Wide Web at http://www.chelseahouse.com

Text design by Annie O'Donnell
Cover design by Ben Peterson

Printed in the United States of America

Bang FOF 10 9 8 7 6 5 4 3 2 1

This book is printed on acid-free paper.

All links and Web addresses were checked and verified to be correct at the time of
publication. Because of the dynamic nature of the Web, some addresses and links
may have changed since publication and may no longer be valid.

*The views expressed in this book are Dr. Adams' alone and not necessarily those of
the City of New York.

Table of Contents

Introduction to Forensic Anthropology

On the 4th of July in 2005, a couple was walking along an access road on Randall's Island in New York City. The man observed a bone near the side of the road and playfully tossed it at his girlfriend. They then became concerned that the bone might actually be human and called the police. Detectives from the New York City Police Department and investigators from the Office of Chief Medical Examiner responded to the scene and noticed other bones scattered in the area that they believed to be human. At this point, the location was treated as a crime scene and a call went out for anthropological assistance. It became of critical importance to determine first, if the bones were indeed human, and second, if they were of **medicolegal** significance, that is, if they might be part of a recent crime or missing person case.

The analysis of human skeletal remains within the medicolegal context is called **forensic anthropology,** and those who practice it are forensic anthropologists. Large cities such as New York City may have a forensic anthropologist on staff who works for the medical examiner's office. In other cases, a forensic anthropologist may work at a university and serve as a consultant on call for various agencies.

Once the forensic anthropologist arrived on the Randall's Island scene, it was immediately determined that the bones were indeed human. Forensic anthropologists are familiar with every feature of the human skeleton, the range of variation between individuals, and the differences between human and nonhuman bones. When bones are complete, the task of determining whether they are human is relatively simple. When the bones are fragmentary, however, it can be a much more challenging task. In this case, both intact and fragmentary bones were observed, some on the surface and some slightly buried. To complicate matters, there were also bones in the vicinity that were identified as nonhuman. The human bones were associated with rubble such as bricks, concrete, metal, and charcoal, which suggested everything was secondarily deposited from another location. In an undisturbed (or primary) burial, the bones would still have been **articulated**. This means that the anatomical location of the bare bones would be exactly the same as when flesh was present. In this case, the lack of articulation was a clear indication that the person (or persons) represented by the bones did not die at this specific location, but the remains were transported there after death and decomposition (i.e., secondarily).

In order to document the location of the bones and any associated evidence (such as clothing), a sketch map was made of the area. Standard archaeological equipment, including shovels and trowels, was used to excavate the site thoroughly. During excavation, all dirt was placed through wire mesh sifting screens in order to recover small items, such as teeth, that might not be readily apparent. This process is exactly the same as a small archaeological excavation that might be undertaken on a prehistoric site. After the recovery effort was complete, the bones were transported to the Office of Chief Medical Examiner in Manhattan for anthropological analysis.

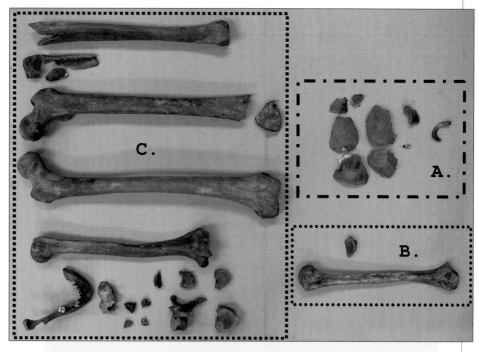

FIGURE 1.1 Bones and teeth discovered on Randall's Island in New York City are arranged into groups according to age *(A = child; B = adolescent; C = adult).*

Figure 1.1 shows the human bones recovered from the site at Randall's Island. To the untrained eye, it may be difficult to state conclusively that these bones are even human. Even to someone familiar with the human skeleton, the bones may appear consistent with one very incomplete and fragmentary skeleton at first glance. A closer analysis of the bones and teeth reveals that there is much more to the story. For example, there are duplicated portions of two right tibiae (shin bones), indicating that more than one person is represented. There are also skeletal and dental indicators that show people of different ages and sizes are represented. This is an example of **commingling**. Commingling means that the bones of more than one individual are mixed together in the same context. In this instance, analysis revealed that there were bones and teeth from a child around 3 years old, the bones of a teenager around 16 years old, and the bones of at least two adults. The **minimum number of individuals (MNI)** is an indicator of the least number of individuals found at a site; in this case, a minimum of four people are represented by the remains. The condition of the bones indicated that they were quite old. Some of these indicators included the complete lack of soft tissue and decompositional odor. The bones were also very dark brown in color and had deterioration of the cortical, or exterior, surface, suggesting that they had been buried for an extended period of time. Another critical clue to consider was the context of their discovery, in which the bones were mixed in with construction debris. There was no sign of any kind of trauma to the bones, only damage that occurred **postmortem,** or after death.

Taken as a whole, the evidence in this case strongly suggested that the bones and teeth originated from a disturbed cemetery, one probably impacted during a construction project, and that construction debris associated with the project was dumped on Randall's Island. These findings were obviously of great importance, since law enforcement officials were then notified that this was not a crime scene involving a multiple homicide or missing persons case. The remains were determined to be not of medicolegal significance, a report of findings was generated, and the case was closed.

OVERVIEW OF FORENSIC ANTHROPOLOGY

Forensic anthropology is a component of **physical anthropology**, the study of human populations from a biological and evolutionary perspective. Physical anthropology is itself a subdiscipline of anthropology, the study of human beings, both their physical characteristics and the nonbiological characteristics that are collectively called culture. Forensic anthropology uses the methods and goals of physical anthropology to study questions of medicolegal significance. In doing this, forensic anthropologists often work with pathologists, homicide detectives, and dental specialists called **forensic odontologists** to identify a decedent, the time of death, and any evidence of foul play.

This book will focus specifically on the applied science of forensic anthropology and provide a general introduction to the many facets of a forensic anthropologist's job. The job of a forensic anthropologist may start at the scene of a crime and involve the recovery of remains using archaeological techniques. To this end, forensic anthropologists need to be able to "read" the soil and recognize subtle signals that may be indicative of a secret or clandestine burial. Once discovered, meticulous recovery techniques must be used to excavate a buried body in order to ensure that the location is documented and that no evidence is lost. Once the bones are back at the laboratory, the forensic anthropologist uses his or her detailed knowledge of the anatomy and biology of the human skeleton to glean clues that can be used to tell about the person during his or her life and after his or her death. Was the person male or female? How old was the person when he or she died? How tall was the person? Did he or she suffer from any disease or past injury? What was the person's race or ancestry? How did he or she die?

The field of forensic anthropology is relatively new. The American Academy of Forensic Sciences (AAFS), which is the premiere forensic organization in the United States, traces its beginnings to 1948.[1] The AAFS is composed of forensic scientists from numerous specialties (e.g., pathology/biology, criminalistics, odontology, and toxicology) and has been publishing leading scientific research papers in its journal, the *Journal of Forensic Sciences*, since 1956.[2] In 1972, physical anthropology became a recognized section within the AAFS, and in 1978, the American

Board of Forensic Anthropology was created to certify forensic anthropologists.[3]

Many credit W.M. Krogman's "Guide to the Identification of Human Skeletal Material," which appeared in a 1939 FBI Law

Subdisciplines of Anthropology

Anthropology is a diverse field of study that includes many specialties, or subdisciplines, that usually fall under the areas of cultural anthropology, archaeology, linguistics, or physical anthropology. The one thing that all anthropologists have in common is that they are interested in the study of human beings. Cultural anthropologists are interested in societies and tend to focus their studies on the lives and social practices of contemporary peoples. Archaeologists, on the other hand, use clues contained in evidence that is buried in the ground to understand past cultures. Linguists study the history and structure of language. Physical anthropologists study human variation, often with a keen interest in evolutionary history. A major component of physical anthropology is the study of the human skeleton, or **human osteology**. Experts in the study of the human skeleton, human osteologists, may apply their skills to the fossilized remains of ancestral humans (paleoanthropology), the study of populations through their dead (biological anthropology or paleodemography), or the analysis of human remains within the medicolegal context (forensic anthropology). Regardless of whether the skeleton is fossilized, prehistoric, historic, or modern, many of the goals of an osteological analysis are the same: to reconstruct as much as possible about a person's life from a thorough examination of his or her bones after death.

Enforcement Bulletin, as the start of the modern era of forensic anthropology. This work took the field of physical anthropology and applied the techniques to the forensic context, specifically, the medicolegal identification of individuals from their skeletal remains. Dr. Krogman's work was the first to be written by an anthropologist specifically for law enforcement, and it marked an important step in the establishment of forensic anthropology in the United States. In his paper, Dr. Krogman outlined how the main components of the biological profile (age, race, sex, and stature) are determined from bones. His paper was the main reference source for many years until he published his classic book *The Human Skeleton in Forensic Medicine* in 1962, which was the first major textbook in forensic anthropology.

Forensic anthropology is a very specialized field, but it can be critical in the resolution of some of the most challenging medicolegal cases. This book will detail many of the skills that a trained forensic anthropologist brings to an investigation. Chapter 2 will begin with a basic overview of the key terminology used by forensic anthropologists and will present some job opportunities and applications within the field. Chapter 3 will present some of the techniques and procedures used in the search and recovery of human remains. Chapters 4 and 5 will cover the portion of a forensic anthropologist's analysis relating to the biological profile: the determination of age, race/ancestry, sex, and height from the skeleton. Chapter 6 will highlight the interpretation of bone trauma, in addition to addressing decomposition rates and the determination of time since death. Chapter 7 will explore some analytical challenges, specifically those relating to species identification, fragmentation, and commingling. Chapter 8 will close the book by discussing how a positive identification of a missing individual can be achieved.

2 Applications and Basic Terminology

Forensic anthropology has a diverse range of applications, and every year more and more agencies are acknowledging the skills that a forensic anthropologist can provide to a wide range of circumstances. Most undergraduate college degrees in anthropology require that a variety of courses are taken, including topics in cultural anthropology, archaeology, linguistics, and physical anthropology. Students begin specializing and focusing on forensic anthropology in graduate school. Almost without exception, practicing forensic anthropologists have a minimum of a master's degree in anthropology, while most have a doctoral (Ph.D.) degree. A master's degree generally requires 2 to 3 years of college after the bachelor's degree. The doctoral degree requires several more years after completion of the master's degree, meaning that a total of 10 years of college is a general estimate of the amount of time required. During the master's and doctoral coursework, advanced classes such as human osteology, human gross anatomy, and forensic anthropology are taken. During this time, the graduate students work with their faculty members to develop research topics that address important forensic topics, such as time since death, trauma interpretation, or age at death, to name a few.

While the coursework involved in training to become a forensic anthropologist is crucial, it is also essential to get as much hands-on experience as possible. This is best attained by volunteering through internship programs as soon as possible. Archaeological experience is also a necessity, and summer field schools are a great way to learn the skills involved with excavation and documentation. Excavating a prehistoric or historic site is a rewarding way to gain valuable experience that can be applied to the recovery of evidence at modern crime scenes.

In general terms, most practicing forensic anthropologists are employed in a university setting, medical examiner or coroner offices, human rights organizations, or the Department of Defense laboratory tasked with identifying missing U.S. military personnel.

ACADEMIA

Most practicing forensic anthropologists work in the university setting as professors. Other professionals may be employed by anthropology departments in museums, such as the Smithsonian Institution's National Museum of Natural History. In this capacity, the job of these individuals is not primarily to work in the field as forensic anthropologists but rather in capacities including teaching, research, or curation and maintenance of collections. They may work as consultants on an as-needed basis for law enforcement agencies, medical examiners, or coroners in their geographic area. These practitioners are of critical importance in training the next generation of anthropologists and in spearheading research projects. For example, the University of Tennessee and the University of Florida have been two of the premiere facilities for training in forensic anthropology, and their students and faculty have been responsible for some of the leading research projects. As the interest in and enthusiasm for the forensic sciences grows, more and more universities are adopting programs that include training in forensic anthropology.

MEDICAL EXAMINER OR CORONER OFFICES

In the United States, there are two systems that handle medico-legal investigations of death: medical examiners and coroners. Medical examiners are usually physicians who are trained in forensic pathology and have expertise in performing forensic autopsies. Coroners, on the other hand, are elected officials that do not need to have any medical training (commonly, they are funeral directors). A coroner will consult with a forensic pathologist when he or she determines that it is warranted. Each state has its own laws relating to either a medical examiner or coroner system. Some crime laboratories and medical examiner offices in the larger U.S. cities may employ a forensic anthropologist as part of their full-time staff. This is possible in such areas as New York City because of the large quantity of casework that comes through the doors. For smaller jurisdictions, there may not be the caseload to justify the hiring of a staff forensic anthropologist, and consultants will be utilized as needed. As employees or consultants for law enforcement or the medical examiner system, forensic anthropologists are an important component of the overall "crime-solving team." While forensic pathologists are experts in the interpretation of soft tissue (skin and vital organs), the forensic anthropologist is the expert on teasing out the clues from the hard tissue (that is, the skeleton) related to identification efforts or trauma interpretation. Together, the medical examiner or coroner and the forensic anthropologist collaborate and use their respective expertise to solve some of the most challenging cases of medicolegal importance.

HUMAN RIGHTS ORGANIZATIONS

Other employment opportunities for forensic anthropologists exist in organizations that deal with human rights issues across the globe. Human rights organizations are often involved in the recovery and identification of victims of genocide. The organizations that investigate these crimes are often composed of international scientists. Some active groups in this field include the Argentine Forensic Anthropology Team (Equipo Argentino de Antropología Forense), Physicians for Human Rights, the Guatemalan Forensic Anthropology Foundation (Fundacíon de Antropología Forense de Guatemala), the International Criminal Tribunal for the former Yugoslavia (ICTY), the International Commission on Missing Persons (IC-MP), and the International Forensic Centre of Excellence for the Investigation of Genocide (INFORCE). Their work is divided between careful archaeological fieldwork to excavate clandestine graves and meticulous laboratory work to document trauma and attempt to identify missing individuals.

The work of the human rights groups can be extremely challenging on many levels. Not only are they working in potentially hostile environments, but the job of identification can be especially problematic due to the lack of **antemortem**, or before death, records in many instances. The work of these groups is of obvious importance to the families of the missing, but it is also critical to the prosecution of those responsible for the atrocities. Forensic anthropologists have worked across the globe, in countries such as Argentina, Guatemala, the former Yugoslavia, Rwanda, Cambodia, and Iraq, to name just a few.

PERSONAL ACCOUNT

A leader in human rights investigations, Luis Fondebrider of the Argentine Forensic Anthropology Team, provides a personal account of a recovery he conducted in Argentina.

Forensic Anthropology and Human Rights Investigations

The old and faded photograph on the table showed a smiling young man in a plaza. His clothes and the setting suggested another time. I was sitting with María Medina, the 68-year-old mother of Pedro. Her son was 22 years old at the time of the photo. A few days after the photo was taken, Pedro was kidnapped by a military unit from the Argentinean dictatorship, joining the long list of disappeared persons who were never heard from again.

From 1976 until 1983, during the last military dictatorship in Argentina, approximately 10,000 people believed to be a threat to the military government were kidnapped and "disappeared" by the armed forces. The vast majority were young people, including students, workers, and others who opposed the dictatorship. After being kidnapped, no one ever heard from them again, leaving their families and friends in anguish and pain. After 1983, when democracy returned to Argentina, the country began to thoroughly investigate and begin to learn what happened (Figure 2.1).

Twenty-eight years later, María told me about her desperate search in military and police units, the lack of any answer from military authorities about where her son was, and the anguish and pain of long nights of waiting. At the same time, María told me about her son, who was 172 cm (about 5 ft 8 in) tall, who did not have any health problems but had broken the bones of his right wrist playing soccer, who also had a pair of dentures and two root canals in his upper teeth. There were no dental records about this, since the work was done more than 28 years ago. Nevertheless, I told her that the information that she gave us was very useful to try to identify the body that we were going to exhume the following day in the city cemetery. To add to this information, I took a blood sample from her so that we could conduct a genetic analysis if it was necessary.

FIGURE 2.1 The Argentine Forensic Anthropology Team (EAAF) has helped people in Latin America, Africa, Europe, and Asia to find the remains of their loved ones, give them an appropriate burial, and bring closure to relatives. The evidence collected about the identities of the bodies and the causes and manners of death also have served as scientific proof in criminal proceedings brought against those alleged to be responsible for the crimes. In this photograph, EAAF team members work at a mass gravesite in Argentina.

The following day, a warm November morning in Buenos Aires, a group of forensic archaeologists and anthropologists met in a quiet part of the local cemetery at a grave with a simple wooden cross with the inscription NN, "no name." Using traditional archaeology techniques, we began to exhume the grave, and little by little uncover a skeleton. Usually an archaeologist's work includes trying to recover human remains and materials from cultures that existed long ago, but in our case, the shovels, trowels and other small tools were applied to exhume the bones of a person who not only was around the same age as we were, but was a peer who could have been our neighbor. In addition, the bones most likely belonged to someone who was illegally executed in a clandestine detention center only a few years before, and not a person who died of a sickness.

María and part of her family were present. They did not approach the grave but we felt them around us. The sound of the earth on the shovels and the tools to remove the earth mixed with their sobs. Even the grave diggers, veterans of daily death, kept a respectful silence around us. After five hours of work, we exposed a complete skeleton with three bullets near the cervical vertebrae and two bullets near a shattered cranium. María asked to see the grave. Her pain was infinite.

The bones have been taken to the laboratory to establish a biological profile and try to find similarities with the information that María gave us. This can take many months, depending on the scientific techniques we need to use. Nevertheless, we have taken an important step in the work of returning the identity to a person who was robbed of his identity. Although we still do not know if this is the body of Pedro, María feels that she may be able to begin to close the cycle of anguish and uncertainty that she has lived with for nearly 30 years.

Luis Fondebrider,
Argentine Forensic Anthropology Team (EAAF), 2006

IDENTIFICATION OF U.S. MILITARY PERSONNEL

Another role for forensic anthropologists is in the search for U.S. service members missing as a result of wars and past conflicts. The Joint POW/MIA Accounting Command (JPAC) is responsible for the recovery and identification of missing U.S. soldiers, sailors, airmen, and marines from past conflicts (*see table below*). JPAC is composed of over 400 individuals, both military personnel and civilian employees. The Central Identification Laboratory (CIL) is the scientific contingent of the organization and is the largest forensic anthropology laboratory in the world. Currently, the CIL employs around 30 civilian anthropologists, all with backgrounds in archaeology and/or forensic anthropology. The roots of the CIL date back to the effort to recover and identify American dead in World War II. Today, the laboratory is located at Hickam Air Force Base on the island of Oahu in Hawaii.

The mission of the CIL is twofold: recovery and identification. The recovery portion of the effort is oftentimes the most challenging and demanding part of the job. Recovery missions take the teams to some of the most remote locations on earth and subject them to grueling conditions. Teams may live in tents in the jungle for upwards of a month while excavating sites believed to contain the remains of missing military personnel. Once human remains and personal effects are recovered, they are transported back to the laboratory in Hawaii. At this point, it is the job of the forensic anthropologists, forensic

Missing U.S. Service Members*	
World War II (1941–1945)	78,000
Korean War (1950–1953)	8,100
Vietnam War (1961–1975)	1,800
Cold War (1945–1991)	120
Gulf War (1991)	1

*Values are approximate as of 2004.

odontologists, and DNA analysts to assess the available evidence in order to make an identification. In recent years, the CIL identifies, on average, between one and two individuals each week.

BASIC FORENSIC ANTHROPOLOGY TERMINOLOGY

In order to understand the basics about forensic anthropology, it is necessary to be familiar with the major bones that compose the human skeleton. In all, there are usually 206 bones in the adult skeleton. The bones of the head (cranium, inner ear, mandible, and hyoid) consist of 29 different bones. The bones below the head, the **postcranial skeleton**, account for the remaining 177 bones. A child's skeleton is composed of many more bones, since each element may be composed of several separate parts that have not yet fused together. For a forensic anthropologist, it is not only essential to know the names of all the bones but also critical to be intimately familiar with all of the landmarks and features of each one. It is also essential to be familiar with the growth and development of the human skeleton. Expertise in skeletal anatomy makes it possible to recognize anomalies that may be critical in the resolution of a case. This section will highlight some of the major bones, landmarks, and terminology associated with forensic anthropology.

The **cranium**, or skull without the lower jaw, is a complex structure that is important for the determination of age, ancestry, and sex from a skeleton (Figure 2.2). The different bones of the cranial vault include the parietals, temporals, frontal, occipital, and the sphenoid. These bones are connected via irregular interlocking joints called **sutures**. The main sutures of the cranial vault are the coronal (between the frontal and parietals), sagittal (midline of the cranium between the parietals), squamosal (between the temporals and parietals), and lambdoidal (between the occipital and parietals).

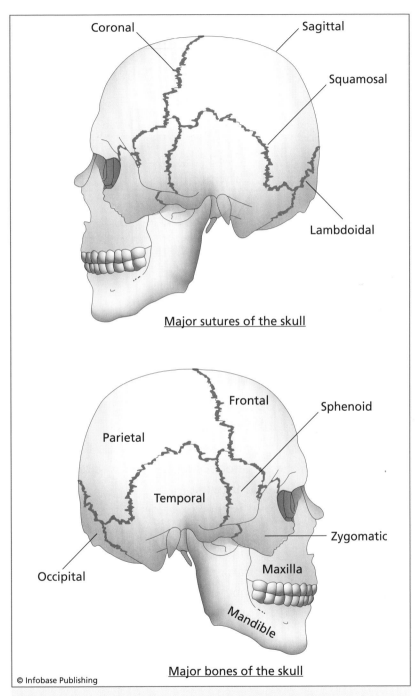

Major sutures of the skull

Major bones of the skull

© Infobase Publishing

FIGURE 2.2 Major bones and sutures of the cranial vault.

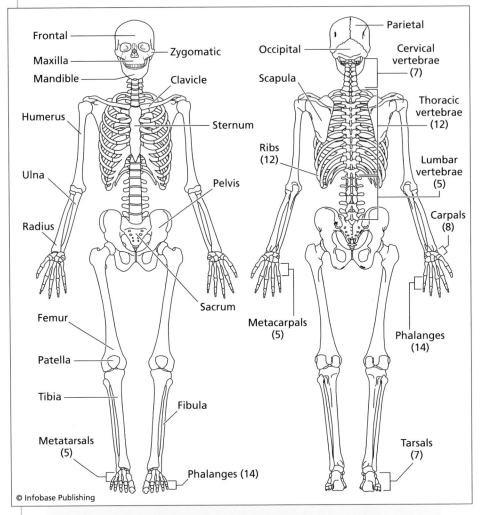

FIGURE 2.3 Major bones of the human skeleton.

The postcranial skeleton is divided into the bones of the torso and limbs (Figure 2.3). The bones of the torso include the ribs, vertebrae, scapulae, clavicles, sternum, pelvis, and sacrum. The bones of the pelvis (hip bones) are some of the most important bones for an anthropological analysis. The pelvis is composed of three portions, the *ilium*, the *ischium*, and the *pubis*, each one of which contains information that may be critical to the determination of age at death or sex in adults. The limbs include the bones of the arms and legs (the humerus, radius, ulna, femur, tibia, and fibula). Most of the bones of the arms and legs are referred to as *long bones* due to their shape.

There is specific terminology used in order to describe precise locations or portions of bones. In order to visualize these terms, it is necessary to think of the skeleton in **anatomical position** (Figure 2.4). Anatomical position means that the person is standing (or laying on his back) with his arms at his sides, palms forward, and with his thumbs to the outside. When the body is in anatomical position, none of the bones cross each other, and it is possible to consistently describe their relationships with other bones. For example, the **proximal** humerus refers to the uppermost portion of the arm near the shoulder joint, while the **distal** humerus refers to the lowermost portion of this bone near the elbow. When referring to portions of the cranium, the top of the head would be referred to as **superior**, while the bottom would be **inferior**. The front of a bone is the **anterior** surface, while the back is the **posterior** surface. Picture the location of the two bones in the forearm: the radius and the ulna. The radius is **lateral** in relation to the ulna (i.e., away from the body's midline), and the ulna is **medial** in relation to the radius (i.e., toward the body's midline).

Other basic terminology describes features, landmarks, and developmental components of bones. A bump or protrusion may be described as a *tuberosity, tubercle, trochanter,* or *process*. All four of these terms mean basically the same thing but are used to describe various bony landmarks, such as the greater trochanter of the femur or the styloid process of the radius. Conversely, a depression may be referred to as a *fossa* or *notch*, such as the glenoid fossa of the scapula that joins (or articulates) with the head

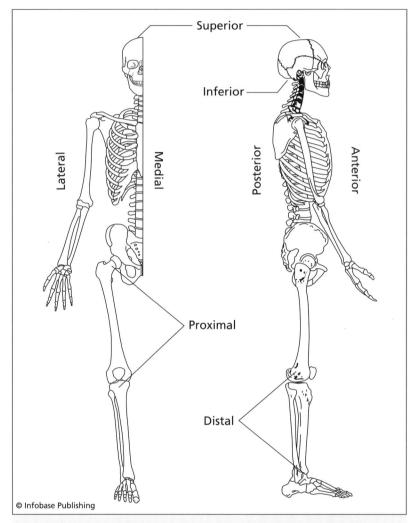

Superior

Inferior

Lateral

Medial

Posterior

Anterior

Proximal

Distal

© Infobase Publishing

FIGURE 2.4 Terms used for anatomical orientation are detailed in this illustration. These terms, such as *proximal*, *distal*, *anterior*, and *posterior*, allow forensic anthropologists to specify the exact location or portion of a bone.

of the humerus. All of the long bones have holes that connect the exterior surface of the bone with the interior surface. These holes are called *foramina* (singular is foramen), and they allow passage of blood vessels through the bones. Some foramina are very distinctive in their shape and location, and can be important for identifying fragmentary bones to a specific element.

There are terms that describe specific portions of long bones. The **diaphysis** is the shaft of a long bone, while the **epiphysis** is a cap that fuses to the shaft. In children, the epiphyses are not fused to the diaphysis, allowing for growth to occur. Because bone growth and development is predictable, observation of the degree of fusion between the various epiphyses and diaphyses is instrumental in the determination of age at death, as will be discussed in Chapter 4. Finally, there are two important terms to describe the morphological size of bones and bony features: **robust** and **gracile**. Robust indicates that something is very large (commonly associated with males), while gracile signifies that it is very small or slight (usually associated with females). In order to accurately use the terms *robust* and *gracile*, it is necessary to comprehend the scope of human variation (for example, a gracile femur may appear extremely large to someone not familiar with human skeletal anatomy).

3

Recovery Procedures

Usually when someone hears the term *archaeology,* it either invokes images of Indiana Jones, with whip at the ready, encountering death-defying situations in exotic lands, or, conversely, dust-covered scientists meticulously digging in the dirt with small picks and brushes uncovering ancient artifacts. Of the two, the second scenario is more accurate. Archaeologists are experts at finding buried evidence, usually of past cultures, in order to better understand these groups from the materials that are left behind. It is critical for archaeologists to be experts at locating, excavating, and documenting this evidence. The same importance can be ascribed to processing evidence at a crime scene, and it is for this reason that most forensic anthropologists also have experience with archaeological techniques. There are three basic components that forensic anthropologists draw from the field of archaeology: site location, excavation, and documentation.

SITE LOCATION

The ability to "read" the soil is essential in the search and recovery of any type of site, and forensic anthropologists employ different techniques depending on the site parameters. In order to perform an initial search for a clandestine (hidden) grave, it may be possible to interpret the soil using either high-tech or rudimentary techniques. For example, if investigators believe that the body of a missing person has been buried within a large field, it may be feasible to use high-tech equipment like ground penetrating radar (GPR). GPR transmits high-frequency radio waves into the ground and creates a map of underground objects or disturbances in the soil, such as a buried body. Use of this type of equipment is extremely helpful, but it is obviously dependent on access to funding and skilled personnel who know how to operate the equipment and interpret the data. The same site may also be searched with a simple soil probe, which is little more than a pointed metal rod that is pushed into the ground. With the soil probe, the operator is simply attempting to "feel" for differences in the soil instead of relying on the electronic equipment.

Evidence of plant and soil disturbance is one of the best ways of visually locating a clandestine grave. Once a hole is dug into the ground, that area will be distinct from the surrounding soil. On the surface, there may be subtle indications of a recent grave based on variation in vegetation or topography. For example, when a grave is dug, it will disrupt the existing vegetation and initiate a new succession of plant life. As a result, a keen eye may be able to notice variation in the vegetation between the disturbed and undisturbed areas, especially soon after the burial takes place.

Topographically, once a grave is back-filled with dirt, it will be mounded higher than the surrounding surface. Over time, the soil settles and the body decomposes, resulting in the formation of a concavity, or depression, at the burial site. Two other soil indicators are compaction and color. **Compaction** simply means that the dirt in a disturbed area such as a grave will be looser than the surrounding undisturbed soil. In order to observe variations in soil color, it is necessary to strip off the topmost layer of soil in order to expose an area that is free of vegetation. The color difference is based on the fact that various soil layers will be mixed together when a hole is dug and refilled. For example, you may have a site that has a top layer of rich, dark soil with a high organic component. Underneath may be a somewhat lighter, silty soil. Deeper still, you may encounter an orange-colored layer that has a high clay content. As a result of digging through these distinct layers, the removed soil will subsequently be mixed together as it is used to refill the hole. In turn, the color of the soil in the burial pit (fill dirt) will be distinct from the surrounding undisturbed soil (Figure 3.1). In most cases, the mixed soil will be darker than the surrounding soil. Evidence of burial pits based on variation in soil color and compaction will remain for a very long time.

EXCAVATION

In archaeology, the **law of superposition** states that as layers of soil accumulate, the deeper layers (and the items associated with these layers) are older than the ones encountered above them. The study of soil layers is called **stratigraphy**. Burial pits disturb these **strata** (soil layers) and create a new, younger feature that now either cuts through or is located above the previously existing levels. If many years pass after the grave is dug, it is possible that a new (and still younger) layer will be naturally deposited over the burial pit. While this relationship may seem simple, it is a very important principle in archaeological excavation, regardless of whether it is in the prehistoric or forensic context.

Once a gravesite (or any type of recovery site with buried evidence) is located, it is of utmost importance that a great deal of time and care is put into the excavation. Excavation of a scene is a destructive process, meaning that you only have one chance to get it right. Thus, it is important that care is taken to preserve and recover

FIGURE 3.1 This example of a burial pit was discovered in September 2001 by removing the topsoil in a cabbage patch. This site was located near the Chosin Reservoir in North Korea, a site of heavy fighting between U.S. and Chinese military forces during the Korean War in late 1950. The dark, cigar-shaped soil within the red dotted oval is the burial pit. It is surrounded by orange-colored soil (original soil color). This pit was approximately 3 x 15 feet (.9 x 4.5 m) in size and contained the skeletons of 12 servicemen.

all relevant evidence from the scene. The excavation strategy will have to be tailored to fit the circumstances of the scene. For example, the recovery of human remains from a building collapse will obviously be handled differently than the recovery of a single body buried in the soil. In one scenario, it may be necessary to use heavy machinery in the excavation process; in the other scenario, it may be possible to excavate the entire scene with hand tools. Regardless of the context, once human remains are encountered, excavation should be completed entirely by hand and with the proper tools.

Use of the proper excavation tools around the body ensures that the bones are not accidentally damaged during excavation. The archaeologist's burial tool kit is not made up of high-tech gadgets. Excavation around the bones is generally completed with wooden implements (for example, sharpened chopsticks), garden trowels, and dental picks. Soil is removed from the bones using paint brushes and whisk brooms. The critical goals are (1) to expose the body for documentation of its orientation and relationship to any associated artifacts and (2) to carefully remove it from the ground without damage. Careless excavation may damage the bones in a manner that masks trauma that may be associated with cause of death. It is also possible that excavation damage could be misinterpreted as trauma (such as a stab wound) associated with the person's death. For this reason, most anthropologists prefer to use only wooden tools, as opposed to metal tools, when excavating in direct contact with bone.

During excavation, all soil that is removed from a burial pit is placed in buckets and subsequently "screened" on site. Screening the soil guarantees that small items, such as teeth or a bullet, that may escape notice during excavation will be discovered and retained as valuable evidence. The screening process is completed by placing all the soil into a box with wire mesh screen as the base. As the soil falls through the openings in the mesh, small items of evidence will be retained. The size of the wire mesh can be tailored to fit the excavation site, but 1/4-inch (6-millimeter) mesh is generally the standard.

DOCUMENTATION

As part of the excavation strategy, meticulous documentation in the form of photographs, notes, and sketch maps are essential.

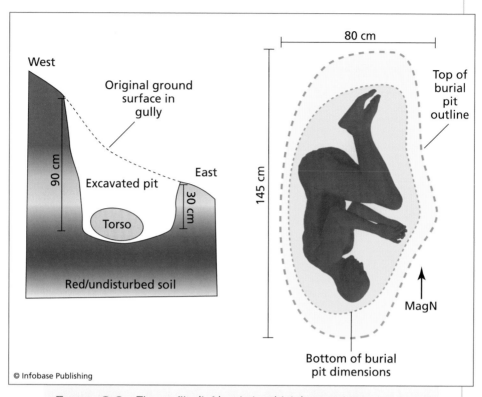

West

Original ground
surface in
gully

90 cm

Excavated pit

East

30 cm

Torso

Red/undisturbed soil

80 cm

Top of
burial
pit
outline

145 cm

MagN

Bottom of burial
pit dimensions

© Infobase Publishing

FIGURE 3.2 The profile *(left)* and plan *(right)* maps above
were drawn to illustrate the location of a homicide victim within a
clandestine grave.

Careful documentation of evidence (bones and associated artifacts) in both horizontal and vertical dimensions allows for some
degree of spatial reconstruction of the site. It is also important
to document information about the associated soil, such as type
(silt versus clay) and color. Maps created as though a person was
above the site and looking down upon it are called **plan maps**.
Maps that look at a cross section of the site, as though the person
made a vertical slice through the area, are called **profile maps**
(Figure 3.2). Together, these maps help to understand the spatial
relationships between the body, the ground, and any associated

items within the grave. Analysis of these data in the laboratory may reveal important relationships that were not fully appreciated in the field.

Finally, taking many photographs and, if possible, video footage is recommended when excavating a crime scene. Film and digital media provide an inexpensive and efficient means of scene documentation. Photographs should not be used in place of notes and sketches, but they are a critically important means to chronologically document a scene in its entirety. The maps and photographs together are also useful visual aids that may be used during court testimony.

JPAC RECOVERY TEAMS

Some of the most complex and challenging recovery sites have been excavated by the teams from the Joint POW/MIA Accounting Command (JPAC) searching for missing U.S. personnel. Each recovery team consists of about a dozen U.S. team members. Some of the different specialists on the team include a forensic anthropologist, a medic, an explosive ordnance disposal technician, a communications expert, a linguist, a life support technician (an expert on aircraft wreckage who can identify equipment items that would have been in direct contact with the pilot), a military officer, and several enlisted military personnel trained in the recovery of human remains. The forensic anthropologist on these missions is usually the sole civilian team member and is responsible for the scientific integrity of the excavation. These archaeological excavations can be large in scope, depending on the circumstances of the loss and may take months to complete and require the work of hundreds of people. Due to the harsh environmental conditions, length of time since death, and the traumatic circumstances of the loss (in the case of an aircraft crash), the only human remains recovered may be small fragments of bone and teeth.

Dr. Robert Mann, deputy scientific director at the JPAC Central Identification Laboratory, provides an account of a recovery that he directed in Vietnam.

Green Berets: Lost and Found

It was a little after midnight on February 7, 1967, when North Vietnamese tanks ripped through the barbed wire and mine fields surrounding the Special Forces camp in Lang Vei, Vietnam. Bullets flew in every direction, grenades and artillery rounds shredded the landscape, and soldiers fought hand to hand as the enemy moved southward. Nothing could stop the Vietnamese soldiers and commandos as they shadowed tanks across the Xe Pon River and made their way to the American outpost at Lang Vei. When the smoke cleared and the fighting was over, more than 200 South Vietnamese soldiers and hill tribe fighters and 10 American Green Berets were dead or missing in action (MIA).

Twenty-six years later, in 1993, investigators at JPAC, the military organization responsible for finding, recovering, and identifying missing Americans from all past wars, intensified their search for the Americans missing at Lang Vei. The search would span more than a decade as teams dug through the rubble hoping to find one Green Beret lost in the underground command bunker and four others last seen fighting "inside the wire" or at the observation bunker outside the camp perimeter (Figure 3.3). Our efforts were rewarded in 2004 when two Vietnamese men digging for scrap metal unearthed two nearly complete skeletons wrapped in a U.S. military poncho.

A search and recovery team escorted the remains, combat boots, dog tags, and uniforms to JPAC for analysis. Using a combination of forensic anthropology and DNA analysis of the bones and forensic odontology of the teeth, scientists were

FIGURE 3.3 Workers remove and sift debris at an excavation site near a former U.S. Special Forces camp in Lang Vei, Vietnam.

able to positively identify the remains as Sergeant First Class Kenneth Hanna and Sergeant First Class Charles Lindewald and send them home to their families. The JPAC had, against all odds, kept its promise to bring home America's troops and upheld its motto, "Until they are home." But with more than 89,000 soldiers, sailors, airmen, and Marines unaccounted for, we still have a lot of work to do.

Robert W. Mann,
Joint POW/MIA Accounting Command, 2005

Biological Profile: Age

After bones are returned to the laboratory setting for analysis, it is up to the forensic anthropologist to analyze the remains and determine as much as possible about the person from whom they originated. Specifically, they analyze the skeletal features that determine the **biological profile.** The "big four" components of the biological profile are age, sex, race/ancestry, and stature (living height). For an unidentified body, each detail of the biological profile will limit the pool of potential matches with missing individuals.

Let's take an example of a body that was discovered in an abandoned building in the Bronx, New York, back in 1989. The individual was in an advanced state of decomposition, with only bones and some mummified skin remaining. Although clothing was present, there was no identifying documents or other items associated with the skeleton. It was the job of the forensic anthropologist to glean as much information from the skeleton as possible to help identify the person and help determine how he or she died. The detailed analysis showed that the bones belonged to a 17- to 23-year-old black male who was approximately 73 inches (185 cm) tall. Additionally, there was a healed fracture with surgical intervention indicating that he had broken his leg in the past and had visited a hospital. Two gunshot wounds to his head indicated that he was murdered. Obviously, this information would be of great help to detectives in the search for the decedent's identity. This chapter will look at how age at death is determined from skeletal remains; Chapter 5 will consider the other components of the biological profile—sex, race/ancestry, and stature.

Determination of age at death from the bones and teeth gets less precise as a person gets older. Growth and development normally occurs at a predictable rate, allowing age-at-death estimates to be quite precise in **subadults** (infants, children, and adolescents). Once growth has ceased, age-at-death estimates in adults are based primarily on degenerative changes or the breakdown of the skeleton. The wear and tear on the human skeleton is variable, resulting in age intervals in adults that are broader than the age intervals encountered with subadults. For example, analysis of the bones and teeth of a child may indicate an appropriate age interval of 3 to 5 years old at the time of death. Analysis of an adult skeleton may be consistent with an individual 35 to 50 years old at the time of death. While more precision in the estimate will help investigators narrow the field of potential candidates, it is dangerous and ill-advised to be overconfident when reporting age ranges. Too narrow of an estimate may not account for the full extent of human skeletal variation and may in turn inadvertently exclude a viable missing person candidate.

DETERMINATION OF AGE IN SUBADULTS

In October 1996, skeletal remains were found in a wooded area outside of Nashville, Tennessee. Law enforcement officials requested assistance from forensic anthropologists at the University of Tennessee with the recovery and analysis of the bones. Once on the scene, the forensic anthropology team was briefed by detectives. They stated that they believed the bones were those of a missing woman whose husband was a prime suspect in her disappearance. Within seconds of looking at the skull, it was possible to tell the detectives that this was definitely *not* the missing woman. Instead, the anthropologists on the scene posed the question, "Are you missing any children from this area?" Based on several skeletal and dental indicators, it was immediately evident that these bones belonged to a young child around 6 to 10 years old at the time of his or her death. At this point, the investigation's course took a dramatic turn and the call went out to gather data on missing children. The remains were eventually identified as a young girl, just shy of her eighth birthday, who had been abducted and murdered, and her body discarded in a ditch.

For determining the age-at-death of all subadults, an assessment of the stage of skeletal and dental development is critical. This may include documentation of the degree of permanent and "baby" teeth formation, the length of bones, and the stage of bone formation and epiphyseal fusion. Each of these important indicators will be addressed.

Dental Development

One of the most reliable indicators of subadult age is dental development. While forensic odontologists work exclusively with the teeth and their supporting structures, this is also the realm of the anthropologist. There is even a specialty within the field of anthropology called dental anthropology, although the usual focus is not forensically oriented. Teeth begin to develop before birth, and they continue in various stages of formation and loss until around 18 years of age. By observing the stage of tooth formation, the stages can be compared to charts and tables to determine the appropriate age interval. Mixed dentition refers to the time period when both **deciduous** (that is, baby teeth) and permanent teeth are represented, which is often the most informative period for making a

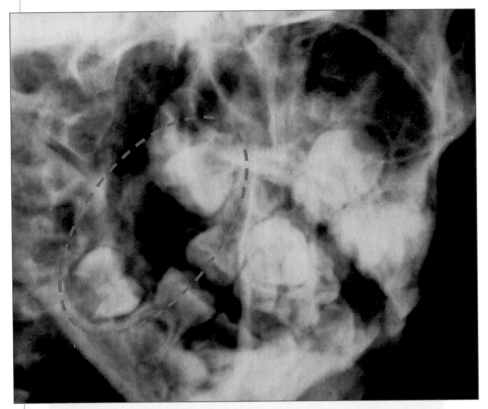

FIGURE 4.1 A dental radiograph can help a forensic anthropologist make an age determination. The development of the permanent molars *(red oval)* is consistent with an age of between 3 and 4 years.

determination of age. In 1991, the body of a decomposed young girl was found in a container along a road in New York City. X-ray analysis of her dental development was used in order to estimate her age (Figure 4.1).

As a rule, both the deciduous and the permanent teeth develop at very predictable rates. One exception to this trend is the development of the permanent third molars, otherwise known as the wisdom teeth. Most commonly, these teeth are present by 18 years of age, but it is not uncommon for them to form much later in life or never at all. A study found that if the third molars are in the early stages of development, the subject is likely to be under 18 years of age, whereas if the third molars are fully formed, one can be reasonably confident that the individual is over 18 years of age.[4]

Epiphyseal Fusion

As the skeleton of a child develops, the bones undergo many changes. As noted in Chapter 2, an immature long bone is composed of a diaphysis (the shaft of the bone) and at least two epiphyses (the bony cap that forms on each end of the bone). The diaphyses and the epiphyses are not initially attached to each other, allowing for the bones to grow in length. At some point, the body determines that the bones have reached their maximum dimensions and growth stops through the fusion of the epiphyses with the diaphyses. Generally, the stages of fusion are described as unfused, partially fused, or fully fused. Fortunately for forensic anthropologists, this epiphyseal fusion occurs at a relatively predictable rate and as a result is critical for an age-at-death estimate.

The medial clavicle (collarbone) is generally the last epiphysis to fuse (Figure 4.2). As a general rule, fusion of the medial clavicle usually commences between 18 and 25 years, and a fully fused medial clavicle usually indicates that the individual is over 25 years of age.[5] In our Bronx case example from the beginning of the chapter, inspection of the bones showed that all of the epiphyses of the arms and legs were nearly fused (some were at the very final stages of fusion), suggesting an age of under 23 years old. Examination of the medial clavicles showed that the epiphyses were just beginning to unite. Together, this information was used to derive the age at death estimate of 17 to 23 years.

Long Bone Length

Long bone length is especially useful for assessing infant remains. Metric data is most applicable to fetal and newborn remains

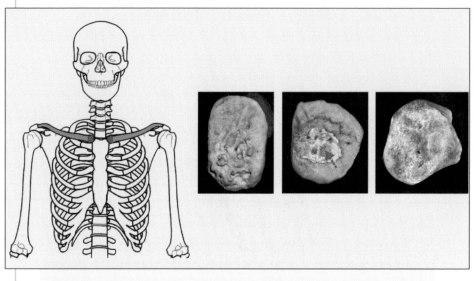

FIGURE 4.2 The medial end of three clavicles are pictured: one unfused *(left)*, one partially fused *(middle, with red arrow marking epiphysis)*, and one that is fully fused *(right)*.

but can also be used with older children. As noted earlier, the skeletons of infants and children consist of numerous epiphyses and cartilaginous precursors that signify very early stages of bone development. Due to the developmental state of the skeleton, the bone measurements taken for age estimates do not include the epiphyses and pertain to only the diaphyses, or shafts. In order to use this technique, the shaft measurements of the unknown child are compared to mean values derived from data on known age children to determine the most likely age-at-death value. Take, for example, a case where a femur shaft was found to have a length of 135 millimeters (5.4 inches). Comparison with published standards shows that this length is most consistent with an individual around 1 year of age. As a person gets older, there is more variation in the size and shape of the long bones, making this technique less reliable.

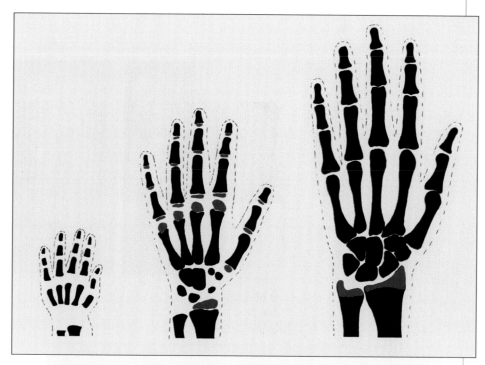

FIGURE 4.3 Stages of hand and wrist development *(birth, 5 years, and 15 years)* in girls is pictured above. Epiphyses are colored gray.

Development of the Hand and Wrist (Radiographic)

As a final example of subadult age estimation techniques, X-ray analysis of the development of the hand and wrist has been used with great success (Figure 4.3). Assessment of the hand X-rays is based on the observation of the development of the carpals (wrist bones) and the various epiphyses of the metacarpals and phalanges (hand and fingers).

DETERMINATION OF AGE IN ADULTS

In early April 2005, an intact skeleton was found in a hidden grave within a storage garage in New York City. The body was

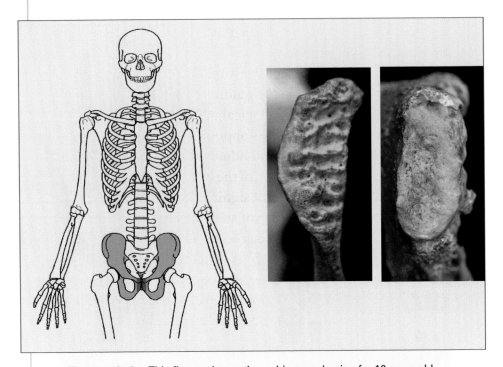

FIGURE 4.4 This figure shows the pubic symphysis of a 16-year-old *(left)* and the pubic symphysis of a person over 50 years of age *(right)*. In the younger individual, pronounced billowing and ridges are present on the surface. Also, note that there is not a distinct rim formed around the face of the symphysis. In the older individual, the billowing and ridges are completely lost and there is a pronounced rim that borders the symphyseal face.

buried almost 5 feet (1.5 meters) below the surface. The search was initiated in the garage based on information provided to detectives by an informant, but it was familiarity with signs of soil disturbance that led to the discovery of its precise location. A forensic anthropological analysis of the remains was completed and the body was determined to be a male between 28 and 38 years of age at death. This age estimate was based on observation of numerous skeletal indicators, particularly features present on his pelvis and ribs. The individual in the grave was subsequently identified as a 34-year-old man who had gone missing in 1986.

As noted previously, adult age estimation is less accurate than with subadults. When assessing adult remains, the techniques are largely based on morphological and degenerative changes of articular (joint) surfaces, as opposed to the developmental changes observed in young individuals. One valuable indicator of age is simply a consideration of the overall health of the individual's bones. Observation of significant arthritic degeneration is an excellent indication of advanced age. Some of these changes may include bony spurs on the vertebral bodies and/or joint surfaces, fusion of numerous vertebrae, and osteoporosis (a loss in bone density). Conversely, a fully developed skeleton that has healthy looking bones without any signs of breakdown is strong evidence that the person is a young adult.

Pubic Symphysis

Perhaps one of the most straightforward techniques of adult age estimation involves the assessment of the **pubic symphysis**. The pubic symphyses are located on the pubic bone of the hip and form the anterior junction between the two halves of the pelvis. Different variations of the assessment have been proposed, but all are based on the changes of the symphyses that occur with age. These transitional changes from youthful to elderly are gradual, allowing for reasonably precise age estimates based on their appearance. In order to analyze the symphysis, representative drawings of the various phases have been published along with their corresponding age intervals. In addition, it is possible to purchase cast exemplars of the different phases, which greatly facilitates comparison with an unidentified specimen.

During the summer of 2005, an unidentified male was found in the Hudson River in New York City. His body was badly decomposed, and it was not possible to visually estimate his age

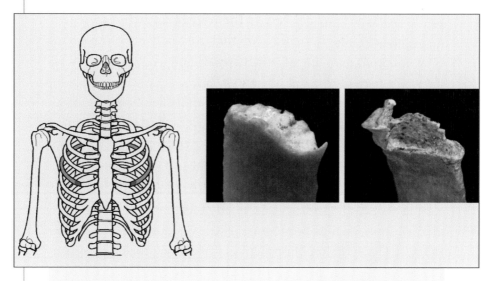

FIGURE 4.5 At left is the sternal end of the fourth rib from a young adult about 19 years of age; at right is an older individual over 60 years of age. Note the bony projections present on the older specimen.

at the time of death. In order to assist the medical examiner, an anthropological analysis was conducted to determine the individual's approximate age. "The pubic symphyses closely matched the early phases of the published techniques, indicating that they were from a young adult (Figure 4.4). Based on the available skeletal evidence, an age range of 20 to 25 years was derived. The person was subsequently identified as a 22-year-old male who was last seen six weeks previously.

Sternal End of the Fourth Ribs

Another useful technique for adult aging uses the form and structure of the sternal end of the fourth rib. Similar to the technique used to analyze the pubic symphysis, phase descriptions of the fourth rib are available along with representative drawings and casts for the male and female exemplars. In young individuals, the sternal end of the fourth rib is basically flat. With age, a pit begins to develop that gradually gets deeper and wider (Figure 4.5). As the pit increases in size, the margins of the pit walls get thinner and more irregular. Eventually, bony spurs will form on the margins of the walls due to the ossification of the costal cartilage that joins the ribs to the sternum. It is important that the age information derived from analysis of the fourth rib is considered in conjunction with the age information from the pubic symphyses, as well as other techniques. This will ensure that the most accurate age estimate is reached.

Biological Profile: Race/ Ancestry, Sex, and Stature

When detectives compile information for missing person reports, one of the primary descriptive characteristics is the missing person's race. For this reason, law enforcement personnel are eager to learn the race of an unidentified skeleton in order to compare this profile with their databases of missing individuals. For a forensic anthropologist, determination of race can be the most complex and frustrating component of the biological profile. For some anthropologists, even the concept of race is problematic, and there is debate over whether or not races exist.[6,7] Regardless of the debate, the concept of race (or at least some kind of classification system) is a central component of a standard forensic anthropology report. The reason for this is that almost every survey or request for personal information will require that individuals assign themselves to a certain group (e.g., white, black, Hispanic, Asian, or Native American). The same is true for missing persons reports. Since our society uses and understands these various categories, they become instrumental in any attempt to find the identity of an unidentified person. For forensic anthropologists, any skeletal evidence that can help assign an unknown person to a specific group can, in turn, narrow the search of the pool of missing individuals. Because of the controversy surrounding this topic, some forensic anthropologists have adopted terms such as *ancestry, cultural affiliation*, or *ethnicity* in the place of "race."

Generally, forensic anthropologists tend to classify individuals into three main groups: **Caucasoid**, or white/European; **Negroid**, or black/African; and **Mongoloid**, or Native American/ Asian. Clearly, these groups do not encompass the diversity of the modern world, and the skeletons of some people do not fit comfortably into these broad classifications. Another consideration is that admixture is a possibility. Admixture refers to a situation where a person has parents that fall into different racial groups. For example, if someone has a Caucasoid mother and a Negroid father, he or she would likely have some skeletal features typical of both groups.

The best area to estimate race/ancestry is from the skull, especially the bones of the face. While features of the postcranial skeleton may also be observed, most forensic anthropologists will first look to the skull and teeth for answers. Many of the differences are relative, meaning that they vary on a scale (e.g., narrow versus wide, or present versus absent) and a familiarity with the range of human variation is essential. What follows is a brief overview of skeletal and dental features associated with the three main racial groups used by forensic anthropologists.

Some general characteristics attributed to Caucasoids include a tall and narrow nasal aperture (opening for the nose). Furthermore, there is a "nasal sill" at the base of the nasal aperture and a prominent nasal spine. This means that there is a thin wall of bone (or sill) along the margin and a prominent outward projection (or spine) of bone at this location. One dental feature commonly associated with Caucasoid individuals is the Carabelli's cusp. This is variably expressed but, when present, is a projection that occurs on the lingual (tongue side) surface of the maxillar first molars. Although not exclusive, this cusp has been shown to occur with the greatest frequency in the Caucasoid group.[8]

While the nasal aperture is tall and narrow in Caucasoids, it is generally short and broad in Negroids. Furthermore, the nasal spine and nasal sill are either very small or completely lacking. Instead of a sill, nasal "guttering" is the feature associated with Negroid individuals. This refers to a trough (or gutter) at the base of the nasal aperture. Another feature of the face associated with black individuals is referred to as *alveolar prognathism*. This refers to a protrusion of the anterior portion of the maxilla (upper jaw)and is a feature generally absent in Caucasoids and Mongoloids. One postcranial feature commonly associated with Negroid individuals is found on the femur (thigh bone). The shape of the shaft is usually very straight in Negroids and exhibits anterior curvature in Caucasoid and Mongoloid individuals.

The classification of Mongoloid is difficult, since it encompasses such a large and diverse population. Whether considering a Native American or a Vietnamese person, both individuals would be classified as Mongoloid. This said, they do share some similar skeletal and dental features. For example, the face of Mongoloid individuals is usually flat in appearance, due in part to the cheekbones that project forward. One of the most prevalent Mongoloid dental features includes shovel-shaped maxillary incisors. This refers to the shape of the biting surface of the front teeth, which have a U-shaped, or shovel-like appearance in cross-section. In Caucasoid and Negroid individuals, the biting surface is usually straight. While variably expressed, the frequency of shovel-shaped incisors has been reported to be as high as 99% in some Asian and Native American groups.[9]

Another technique for racial determination is through the use of measurement data. Measurements of the cranium, called **craniometric data**, can be very informative regarding classification into various racial groups, since these data are able to capture information regarding the relative size and shape of the head. In order to statistically compare the craniometric data from an unknown individual to the craniometric data of a pool of known individuals, a computer program called FORDISC can be utilized. FORDISC runs statistical comparisons based on the available cranial measurement data and assigns an unidentified cranium to a specific group.

Overall, there are no easy answers and few "textbook" cases when determining race/ancestry from skeletal remains. It is a controversial topic, but one that is necessary to the field of forensic anthropology. As long as race/ancestry is included on missing persons forms, there is a need for forensic anthropologists to make this assessment. That said, if the findings are ambiguous, the forensic anthropologist also has to be careful not to inadvertently mislead an investigation.

SEX DETERMINATION

As long as most of the bones are available for analysis, determination of sex from the adult skeleton is generally straightforward and lacks many of the complexities inherent to race/ancestry determinations. In the case of sex determination, there are only two choices: male or female. Interestingly, the skeletal features allowing for determination of sex are not apparent until after puberty. This means that it is nearly impossible (or at least very unreliable) to differentiate a young boy from a young girl based only on their bones. In these instances, clues must be derived from contextual evidence (clothing or hair associated with the remains) or through DNA analysis.

Sex determination from the adult human skeleton can usually be reliably determined through an assessment of features found on the pelvis and cranium (Figure 5.1). In addition, measurement data from the postcranial skeleton can be very informative.

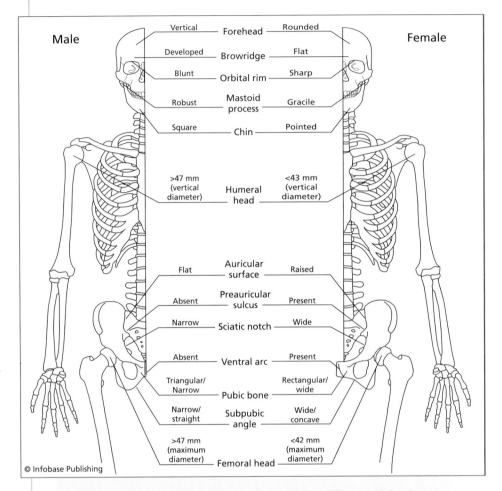

Male		Female
Vertical	Forehead	Rounded
Developed	Browridge	Flat
Blunt	Orbital rim	Sharp
Robust	Mastoid process	Gracile
Square	Chin	Pointed
>47 mm (vertical diameter)	Humeral head	<43 mm (vertical diameter)
Flat	Auricular surface	Raised
Absent	Preauricular sulcus	Present
Narrow	Sciatic notch	Wide
Absent	Ventral arc	Present
Triangular/ Narrow	Pubic bone	Rectangular/ wide
Narrow/ straight	Subpubic angle	Wide/ concave
>47 mm (maximum diameter)	Femoral head	<42 mm (maximum diameter)

© Infobase Publishing

FIGURE 5.1 Forensic anthropologists examine different skeletal features in order to determine an individual's sex.

By far the most telling part of the human skeleton in regard to sex differences is the pelvis. The morphology of the female pelvis is quite distinct from that of the male for one simple reason: childbirth. The female pelvis exhibits some distinctive morphological differences that are related to the ability of the birth canal to accommodate the head of an infant. Studies have shown that sex can be accurately determined from the bones of the adult pelvis upwards of 95% of the time.[10,11] Key areas for observation include the pubis, sciatic notch, and the auricular surface. The sciatic notch is a large concavity located on the ilium, one of the portions of the pelvis. Usually the sciatic notch is very wide in females and narrow in males. Forensic anthropologists refer to the "rule of thumb" when assessing the size of the sciatic notch.[12] If the size of the notch approximates the size of your thumb, the pelvis is likely from a male; if you can comfortably move your thumb back and forth in the notch, the pelvis is likely from a female.

While the pelvis is the best area to determine an individual's sex, the skull may also be used. For these determinations, sex differences are based solely on an assessment of size and robusticity. In general, the male skull will be larger and have more pronounced muscle attachment sites than the female skull. For example, males usually have very prominent (or robust) mastoid processes, projections that serve as muscle attachment sites behind the ears, while females have much smaller (or gracile) mastoid processes. Due to human variation, it is possible for a man to have very gracile features or for a female to have very robust features. In these instances, an analysis of the skull may provide erroneous results, although the pelvis should still be accurate. The bones of the postcranial skeleton will generally be larger, or more robust, in males than females. Studies have found good discriminating power using standard osteological measurements. For example, the size of the head of the femur (thigh bone) alone can classify the sex of individuals with a high degree of accuracy.

STATURE ESTIMATION

Estimating a person's living height, or stature, is usually straightforward and involves the use of calculation of a regression formula. The results are presented as a point estimate of the predicted stature (along with an appropriate margin of error). Because of the speed at which children grow, it is not common to estimate living height from the bones of children (age is far more important in this case). Most stature formulae utilize measurements of fully formed bones. The best skeletal elements to use are the long bones of the arms and legs. In order to measure long bone length, an instrument called an osteometric board is employed. An osteometric board is simply a ruler with one vertical fixed wall and a movable side.

There are two types of stature estimates that can be generated: forensic stature and measured stature. **Forensic stature** refers to self-reported height, for example, from a driver's license. Studies have shown that people tend to embellish their height when self-reporting. For example, research conducted on a sample of college students discovered that there existed a significant difference between a person's measured height and what the person had reported for his or her driver's license.[13] In most instances, the individuals tended to over-report their height on their license. **Measured stature** involves the documentation of living height through the use of a measuring device and is usually recorded by another individual. Measured stature may be found in military records or medical files, for example. There is more precision associated with measured stature than with forensic stature. The forensic anthropologist will have to decide which type of estimate to present, which will depend on the circumstances of the case and the available information. For example, the skeleton of an unidentified person found in New York City will probably need to have forensic stature reported, while it would be appropriate to report measured stature for a skeleton believed to be a missing soldier from the Korean War.

One of the pioneers in the study of stature estimation was Mildred Trotter. Beginning in World War II and continuing with the Korean War, Dr. Trotter used data collected from the skeletonized remains of U.S. war dead to generate her calculations. Dr. Trotter collected metric data from the major long bones during the skeletal analysis of the remains. Once an identification was made, the skeletal data could then be compared to the living stature (measured stature) documented in the military personnel files. The stature formulae resulting from this work are still considered to be some of the best available and are relied upon by forensic anthropologists to this day.[14,15]

Let's take, for example, the skeleton of a white male with a femur length of 47.8 centimeters (18.8 inches). The stature formula for white males is:

$$\text{Stature} = (2.32 \times \text{Length of Femur}) + 65.53$$

Inputting a femur length of 47.8 into the equation results in a predicted stature of about 176.4 centimeters. This value can be divided by 2.54 in order to convert to inches, for an estimate of 69.4 inches, or nearly 5 feet 9 ½ inches. The forensic anthropologist can provide this information to detectives for comparison with missing individuals. Stature estimates are most helpful in cases where the person is unusually short or tall, since the pool of potential matches will be much smaller. For example, in 2004, a skeleton was found buried in an empty lot in Queens, New York. The maximum length of the femur was 55.0 centimeters, which suggests a living height of approximately 6 feet 4 inches. Comparison with the documented statures of several people believed to be have been murdered and possibly buried in the lot made the process of identification much easier. One man was 5 inches taller than any of the others (he was reportedly 6 feet 3 inches tall), which strongly suggested that these bones belonged to him.

6

Assessing Trauma and Time Since Death

Besides the biological profile, a forensic anthropologist is often called upon to assist in the assessment of trauma as well as the time since death. Trauma analysis may reveal evidence regarding injuries that occurred during life or injuries that could be attributed to the individual's cause of death. There are even situations when the trauma occurs after death, such as with dismemberment of a corpse. Regardless of the timing, the bones will retain valuable clues to help decipher these events.

Determination of the postmortem interval, or time since death, is an important aspect of any forensic investigation. This allows investigators to construct a timeline of events relevant to their case.

Specifically, when was the last time the decedent was seen alive, and how long does the state of preservation indicate that he or she has been dead? This is of obvious relevance with a death whose circumstances are unknown, for example, an unwitnessed death (an individual who dies at home alone) or a homicide (a decomposed body that is discovered dumped in the woods).

TIMING OF EVENTS: ANTEMORTEM, PERIMORTEM, AND POSTMORTEM

As part of the anthropological analysis of trauma and time since death, it is very important to consider the timing of events. Three descriptive terms are used for this purpose: antemortem, perimortem, and postmortem. **Antemortem** means "before death." Observation of antemortem skeletal trauma signifies that the bone is healing or has healed. In most cases, this is not related to the cause of death but may be critical in the identification of a missing person. For example, if someone fractured a bone, say his or her tibia, and it subsequently healed, there is likely to be evidence in the form of a bony callous (Figure 6.1). If the person sought medical attention, then X-rays may be available for comparison, which could lead to a positive identification.

Perimortem trauma occurs around the time of death. This term is generally used to describe events such as trauma that occurred very near the time of death and that were likely contributory factors in the death. An example of perimortem trauma would be a gunshot wound without any evidence of healing. A gunshot wound with remodeled (that is, healed) margins would be evidence that it was an antemortem injury that the person survived. It is also possible that, although survivable, the gunshot wound might have triggered other events that eventually resulted in death. An accurate assessment of perimortem trauma is critical in attempting to figure out how a person died and to determine if foul play was involved.

Postmortem means "after death," and observation of changes that occur to the body during this time period are critical in the determination of time since death. In general, postmortem changes are not associated with death and are the result of natural taphonomic processes. Taphonomy is the study of what happens to an organism's remains after it dies, and **forensic**

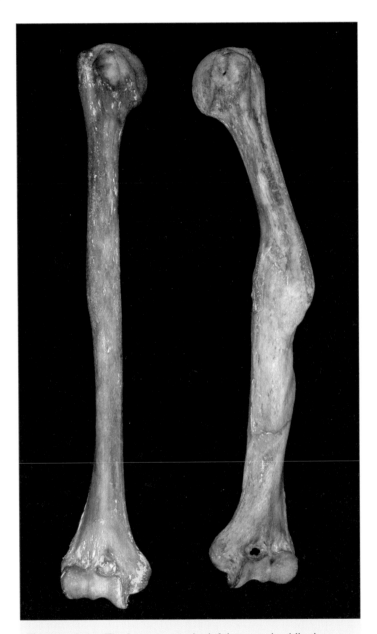

FIGURE 6.1 The humerus on the left is normal, while the humerus on the right has an antemortem (healed) fracture of the shaft. The midshaft bowing of the humerus on the right is the result of a fracture that was never medically treated and set.

taphonomy is the study of the processes and changes that occur between a person's death and the time of the body's discovery. This may consist of soft tissue changes, or it may be more advanced and pertain to the general breakdown and weathering of the bone (Figure 6.2). Additional postmortem changes may result from scavenging by animals. For example, animals such as dogs or rodents may chew and scatter human remains. The critical role of the forensic anthropologist in this scenario would be to recognize that the marks on the bone are the result of dog or rodent teeth (postmortem) and not cut marks (perimortem) associated with death. In addition, taphonomic changes to the body, including animal scavenging, may be instrumental in the determination of time since death.

It is often possible to distinguish between perimortem trauma and postmortem damage by examining the colors of the affected surfaces. For example, if a bone breaks after skeletonization (postmortem), then the color of the fracture margin will be different (usually lighter) than the color of the exterior surface of the bone. If the fracture happens around the time of death (perimortem), then the fracture site margins will be exposed to the same taphonomic forces as the cortical bone. As a result, both areas should be the same color.

Dry bone also fractures differently than "green" (or greasy) bone, which may provide additional evidence as to the timing of the event. In June 1993, a construction worker was clearing vegetation for a new subdivision in Marietta, Georgia, when he found the skeletal remains of an adult female. An anthropological analysis of the disarticulated (i.e., scattered) remains was conducted, and taphonomic indicators were instrumental in reconstructing the details of the case. Variations in bone color showed that damage observed on many of the bones was a postmortem artifact from the machinery, and they did not occur from perimortem trauma associated with the woman's death.[16]

FIGURE 6.2 This figure shows a left femur with marked preservational differences. Notice how the proximal *(right)* portion of the bone is dark in color, while the distal *(left)* portion has been bleached white from exposure to the sun. This is an indication that part of the body was covered or buried and other parts were on the surface and exposed to the elements.

TYPES OF TRAUMA

It is the job of the medical examiner or coroner to determine cause and manner of death, not the anthropologist. The **cause of death** is the disease or injury responsible for initiating the lethal sequence of events, and it is usually based on the medical findings of a doctor. An example would be a gunshot wound of the head or atherosclerotic cardiovascular disease (heart attack). There are numerous descriptive causes that can be recorded on a death certificate, depending on the findings at autopsy. There is less flexibility in the designation of **manner of death,** as it is based on the evidence and the circumstances surrounding a person's death. Usually the manner of death may be classified as natural, accident, homicide, suicide, or undetermined. A gunshot wound of the head would likely be homicide or suicide, while heart disease would be considered natural. If an injury of any kind contributes to death, no matter how minor, the manner cannot be classified as natural. While it is not the responsibility of the anthropologist to determine cause and manner of death, in the case of a skeletonized body, the cause and manner

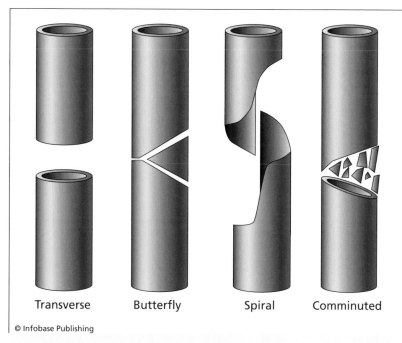

| Transverse | Butterfly | Spiral | Comminuted |

© Infobase Publishing

FIGURE 6.3   Typical long bone fractures.

are likely to be based on the analytical findings provided by the forensic anthropologist.

Most traumatic events can be grouped into three categories: blunt force, sharp force, or gunshot (projectile). Blunt force trauma may result from the impact of an object with the body. For example, a bat, hammer, car, or rock may all inflict blunt force injuries that cause skeletal damage. As a result of the forces acting on the bone, different fracture types are created. For the long bones, some of the more common types of fractures may include spiral, butterfly, transverse, and comminuted (Figure 6.3). Blunt force fractures to the cranium may result in depressed fractures that can preserve the shape of the implement in some cases. Based on an interpretation of the fracture lines, it may be possible to sequence the events (i.e., tell which impact was first, second, and so on).

Gunshot wounds are a special type of blunt force trauma involving the impact of a projectile. The types of injuries can vary based on the caliber, type of projectile, distance, and angle of impact. Distinguishing between entrance wounds and exit wounds, especially on the cranium, is accomplished by observation of internal and external beveling. As a bullet enters the cranium, it will punch out a hole in the bone, leaving a smooth margin on the ectocranial (outside) portion of the cranial vault. As it passes into the inside of the vault, it chips away bone on the endocranial (inside) surface. The result is a defect with smooth margins ectocranially and beveled margins endocranially. Just the reverse occurs as the bullet passes through the opposite side of the head. Defects associated with exits have smooth margins endocranially and beveled margins ectocranially (Figure 6.4). Gunshot wounds to the postcranial skeleton behave similarly in regard to beveling.[17] Often, due to extensive fragmentation, it is necessary to reconstruct the damaged bone during analysis in order to fully observe the characteristics of the wound that are used to determine the bullet's path.

Generally, sharp force injuries are determined to be stab or slash wounds. The difference between the two is that stab wounds are deeper than they are wide, while slash wounds are longer than they are deep. These determinations are often more easily made from soft tissue wounds rather than from marks left on bone. A knife is obviously one of the most common implements associated with sharp force trauma. The blades may take on a variety of shapes, sizes, and styles (e.g., straight vs. serrated). In general, since a knife has a long, thin cutting surface that tapers to a narrow edge, the resulting damage to bone will be V-shaped in appearance. In some instances, it may be possible to differentiate a cut created by a serrated knife from one created by a knife with a straight edge.

Occasionally, a murderer may mutilate the body of the victim. This may be in an attempt to hinder identification efforts or to ease

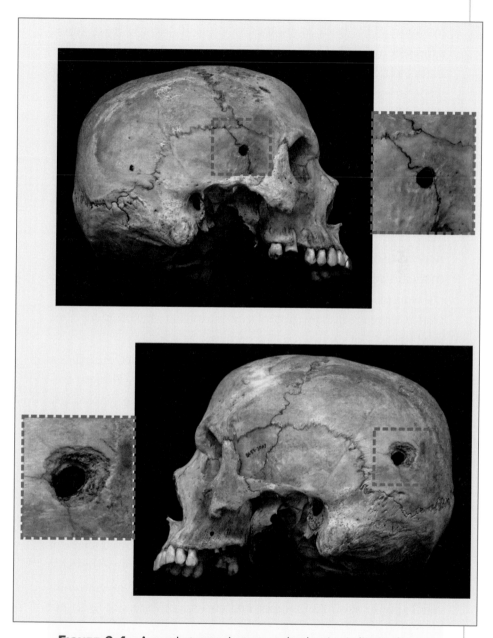

FIGURE 6.4 A gunshot wound entrance *(top)* and exit *(bottom)* are visible on the skull of this homicide victim. Note the absence of ectocranial beveling on the entrance and its presence on the exit.

transport of the body to another location. In these types of cases, a forensic anthropologist may be consulted in the analysis of tool marks left on the bone. Two terms used to describe this type of scenario are *postmortem dismemberment* and *disarticulation*. While there is a fine line between the two terms, disarticulation more accurately describes the removal of body parts at the natural joints (e.g., at the junction between the distal femur and the proximal tibia). Dismemberment is used to describe the process of cutting a body into pieces at any location, for example, in the middle of the femur. Quite often, knives are used for disarticulation since the blade can be used to cut between joints. Both hand and power saws may be used for dismemberment, since they will have an easier time cutting through bones. While there are indications in knife cut wounds to allow differentiation between straight and serrated blades, there are also features of saw marks that may provides clues as to the type of saw used in the process.

A key term in saw and knife mark analysis is **kerf**. A kerf is a groove composed of the walls and floor of a cut mark. The kerf created by a kitchen knife will be very small, while the kerf created by a chain saw will be quite large. A cut that completely bisects a bone will leave only the kerf walls for observation. A "false start" refers to a saw cut that partially passes through the bone but stops short of completely separating the halves. False starts are critically important because the kerf walls and floor are fully retained. The width of the cut formed by the walls and the floor of the kerf will be a close approximation of the blade width. Review of the size and shape of the striations in the kerf walls will provide an indication of the blade characteristics. Some variations may include circular blade, straight blade, power saw, manual saw, and various numbers of teeth per inch on the blades.

Perhaps one of the most distinctive saw types is the chain saw. This is due mainly to the large width of the blade (chain) and the size of the teeth. The resulting lines, or striae, observed in the kerf

FIGURE 6.5 Cross sections of bones showing different saw mark characteristics *(left = chain saw; middle = hacksaw; and right = autopsy saw)* are pictured. Note the variation in striae shape and size between the three.

created by a chain saw will be very large and undulating, especially in comparison with other saw types (Figure 6.5). In early 2005, plastic bags containing body parts were found in a Brooklyn, New York, subway station. An anthropological analysis of the tool marks associated with the dismemberment was requested in order to provide valuable clues to the case. Both legs had been removed at mid-thigh, and it was possible to observe the cutting characteristics on the cross sections of the femora. In addition, there was a false-start kerf on the proximal tibia that allowed for a determination of the blade width. All of the available tool mark evidence indicated that the type of saw used to dismember the body was a chain saw. This information was provided to NYPD detectives and became a critical component in their homicide investigation.

TIME SINCE DEATH

There are changes that occur to the body very soon after death that can provide a very precise postmortem interval. Some of these include stiffness of the muscles (rigor mortis), cooling of the body temperature (algor mortis), and pooling of blood based on gravitational forces (livor mortis). Since these changes are associated with the first 48 hours after death, it would be unusual for a forensic anthropologist to be consulted in such cases. As the putrefactive changes advance, the time since death estimate gets less precise. Estimates at this point are based on the degree of decomposition associated with the body and are more within the scope of a forensic anthropologist's expertise. Depending on the amount of time that passes between death and discovery, a body may be encountered that is fresh, bloated, mummified, skeletonized, or in a combination of these states.

There are many variables associated with decomposition rates. Time is obviously one vital component, but the two most critical are climate and context. Climate is important, since cold weather will slow the decomposition process. If temperatures are low enough, a body may be preserved for years or even centuries. Warm and humid climates will accelerate decomposition rates, and it has been shown that a body can become completely skeletonized in as little as two weeks.[18] Hot and dry climates have the tendency to preserve bodies through natural mummification.

Closely tied in with the climate are the insects that feed on human remains. **Forensic entomology** is a specialty that studies the progression of insects associated with a decomposing body. The presence of insects can be a good indicator for the time of death, since different insects will be present at different stages of decomposition. Most notorious are the flies, which can be observed to land on a body within minutes of death. Also, scavenging carnivores may impact a body, and studies have shown that there is a natural progression associated with carnivore scavenging that can be correlated with time since death.[19,20]

Consideration of the context of a body will greatly affect the time since death estimate. For example, was the body buried, on the ground surface, in the water, in a shaded environment, in direct

FIGURE 6.6 At the Anthropological Research Facility *(pictured above)*, forensic scientists study the decomposition of the human body.

sunlight, in a locked and secured apartment, or in a plastic bag? You can imagine any number of scenarios, each one of which will have an impact on decomposition. It is precisely because of these variables that it is difficult to develop a "cookbook" approach to the interpretation of the postmortem interval. As a rule of thumb, it has been suggested that the degree of decomposition observed on a body on the surface after one week would take two weeks if the same body was placed in water and eight weeks if the body was buried.[21]

THE BODY FARM

One of the most unique forensic facilities in the world is the Anthropological Research Facility (informally called the Body Farm) operated by the Department of Anthropology at the University of Tennessee at Knoxville (Figure 6.6). This is one of the few research facilities where decomposition studies can be performed on actual human bodies placed in a variety of scenar-

William M. Bass, Ph.D.

Every forensic anthropologist, and most archaeologists, own a well-used copy of William Bass's laboratory and field manual *Human Osteology*. In 1971, Dr. Bass took over the anthropology program at the University of Tennessee and became the state forensic anthropologist (Figure 6.7). One question that always perplexed Dr. Bass involved the determination of time since death. It is always one of the first questions asked by law enforcement personnel, and one that Dr. Bass found intriguing. There was one humbling case in particular, noted in his book *Death's Acre*, in which Dr. Bass was asked to offer a time since death estimate for the police. Based on decomposition, Dr. Bass surmised that the individual had been dead for less than one year. Upon further analysis and investigation, it turned out that the body was that of Colonel Shy, a man who had died in 1864 during the Civil War. His grave had been disturbed by looters, but his body was so well-preserved that it appeared to be a recent death. Dr. Bass humorously noted how he missed the time of death in this case by 113 years. This case is an example of why the Anthropological Research Facility, more commonly known today as the Body Farm, is so important. Dr. Bass's research and that of his students at the Body Farm has provided some of the best data regarding time since death estimation that is currently available. Furthermore, the Body Farm is used as a unique training facility to teach students and law enforcement personnel about finding and excavating buried bodies in various states of decomposition.

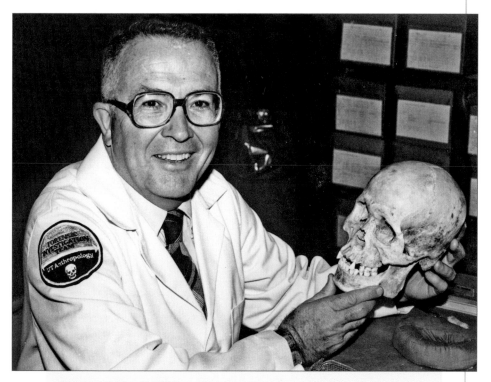

FIGURE 6.7 Dr. William Bass poses with a skull at the University of Tennessee, Knoxville.

ios. This facility was created by Dr. William Bass in 1972 for the specific reason of studying decomposition rates of the human body. The Body Farm initially started as a small plot in a wooded area owned by the University of Tennessee. Today, it is close to an acre in size and is located near the University Medical Center. At this unique facility, human corpses are placed in various environments in order to study the decay process. While obviously very gruesome (and occasionally controversial), the research that has come from studies at the Body Farm has been critical to furthering forensic anthropology. At any point in time, the Body Farm may contain numerous bodies placed in various scenarios, such as on the ground surface, within cars, buried, within water, under concrete, or any other situation that researchers or law enforcement personnel may propose in order to answer questions regarding the decomposition process. Equally as important as the field studies is the comparative skeletal collection that is derived from the decomposition research at the facility. After skeletonization of the bodies, the bones are carefully collected, cleaned, inventoried, and catalogued. The donated skeletal collection contains the bones of hundreds of known individuals. Documentation of the person's life (and death) history is an incredibly valuable research tool for scientists wishing to study the human skeleton.

Analytical Challenges

Although trite, it is safe to say that the only thing that forensic anthropology cases have in common is that none are the same. Every case presents its own set of unique challenges, and many unusual cases become the responsibility of the forensic anthropologist to sort out. The previous chapters have outlined some of the analytical procedures pertaining to mostly intact, complete skeletons. While it is ideal to have pristine bones available for analysis, in reality, this is seldom the case. Quite frequently, the skeleton is fragmentary, poorly represented, jumbled, and eroded. These are but a few of the analytical challenges that a forensic anthropologist may face.

HUMAN, NONHUMAN, AND HISTORIC REMAINS

Sometimes, the role of the forensic anthropologist is as simple as determining whether or not bones are human. This is the first thing that a forensic anthropologist must determine after bones are recovered. Usually bones that are found to be nonhuman are not of medicolegal significance, and the case is closed. When the bones are complete, it is usually straightforward and very easy for an osteologist to differentiate between human and nonhuman remains. However, there are still instances that are quite tricky, since some nonhuman bones closely resemble human ones. This is especially true of the bones from infants and children, since to the untrained eye they may not even look human (Figure 7.1).

In a forensic context, the simple fact that bones are determined to be human does not necessarily mean that they are of medico-legal significance. An example of such a scenario was presented in Chapter 1. In that example, the remains were shown to have most likely originated from a historic cemetery that was disturbed during a construction project. Another such case occurred in Brooklyn, New York, when a homeowner was doing some construction in his basement. While digging, he encountered human skeletal remains and called the police. Forensic anthropologists from the medical examiner's office also responded to the scene and were able to quickly determine that the bones originated from an ancient Native American burial that predated the construction of the homeowner's brownstone building. There were clues in the bones, teeth, and associated soil to indicate that the remains were from an ancient burial and not from a modern crime scene.

Occasionally, police may unexpectedly encounter human remains while serving a search warrant as part of an investigation. This obviously catches the attention of law enforcement personnel, and representatives from the medical examiner's office are usually summoned to the scene. In the most innocent cases, the bones may simply be anatomical teaching specimens or curiosity items that were legitimately obtained (e.g., via Internet sites or specialty stores). There are also scenarios where remains may have been illegally purchased (such as ancient Native American bones) or acquired through illicit means (for example, looted from a cemetery). There are several cases reported each year in the United States regarding "trophy skulls." In most cases, these are associated with past wars in which the skull of an enemy was

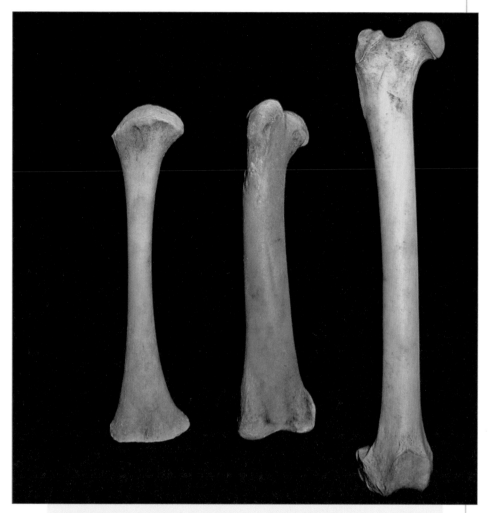

FIGURE 7.1 Comparison of three femora (upper leg bones): newborn human *(left)*, adult chicken *(middle)*, and adult cat *(right)*.

kept as a souvenir of the conflict. Quite frequently, these trophy skulls have names, locations, and dates of the battle written on the bone.

There are also instances where human remains are discovered that have been used for ceremonial purposes. In New York

City, there have been several instances where ritualistic displays of human remains, especially crania, have been found. These are often associated with the black magic sect called Palo Mayombe.[22] Generally, these bones were looted from graves (which is a crime), but the possibility that they may be part of a homicide must always be considered. For example, in April 2005, two crania were discovered outside of an apartment in the Bronx, New York, and police were called. Numerous candles had been burned on top of the crania and there was charring of several areas (Figure 7.2). Anthropological analysis revealed no evidence to suggest that they were part of a recent homicide. The condition of the crania strongly suggested that they were used for ceremonial purposes and that they may have been looted from a cemetery.

FRAGMENTATION

As bones become broken, the job of the forensic anthropologist gets more complicated. As the degree of fragmentation increases, so does the chance that critical skeletal features will be obliterated. It is for this reason that a forensic anthropologist must treat fragmentary bones like a giant jigsaw puzzle and painstakingly reconstruct the pieces as much as possible.

In extreme cases of fragmentation, the determination of whether or not bones are human becomes vastly more complicated. Burning can further fragment and disfigure bone, adding yet another level of complexity to the problem. In some instances of extreme fragmentation and burning, it may even be difficult to determine if the items in question are bone. For law enforcement personnel, and even experienced medical doctors, it is better to be safe than sorry when suspicious bones are encountered and an osteologist should always be consulted.

If fragmentation is so extreme that gross identification of human versus nonhuman bone is not possible, a microscopic

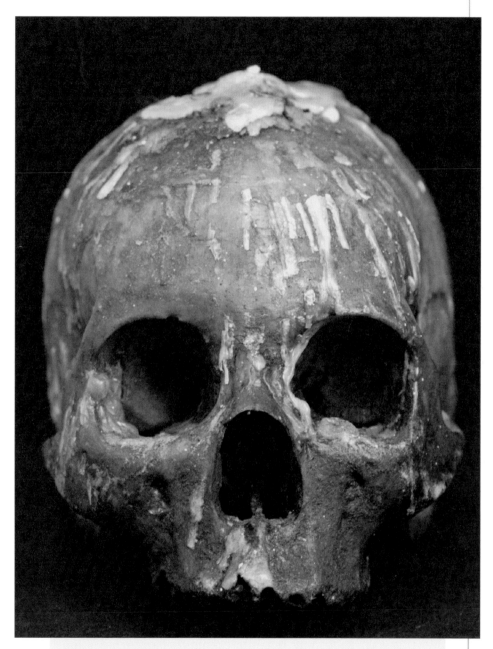

FIGURE 7.2 This ceremonial skull covered in candle wax was recovered outside of an apartment in New York City.

technique can be employed. In this technique, a small section of bone is cut and ground so thin that it is possible to see through it. This sample is mounted on a glass slide and observed under a microscope at a minimum of 50× magnification. The shape of the bone cells may be indicative of nonhuman bone. Compact human bone is composed of oval-shaped morphological structures called osteons. An osteon looks very similar to the cross section of a tree trunk with a central canal and numerous rings surrounding it (Figure 7.3). In contrast, many nonhuman species exhibit micro-structures that appear like stacked bricks called plexiform bone. However, this technique is not foolproof, since some nonhuman animals (e.g., large dogs, bovines, and nonhuman primates) also exhibit osteons.

COMMINGLING

In forensic anthropology, commingling is a term used to signify that the remains of more than one person are mixed together. Generally, commingling occurs as a result of a disaster or when bodies are placed together in a mass grave. In transportation disasters, such as an airplane crash, there is quite often body fragmentation that results in commingling. In a mass grave, bodies are usually placed in the ground in close proximity to each other and without any organization. As a result, recovery of these individuals is quite complicated and some degree of com-mingling is likely to occur, especially with the smaller bones of the hands and feet.

One of the most tragic events in U.S. history was the terrorist attack on the World Trade Center towers in New York City on September 11, 2001. Although this is usually thought of as a single event, it was really four separate events that occurred almost simultaneously. There were two airplane crashes and two build-ing collapses. As a result of these events, commingling of human

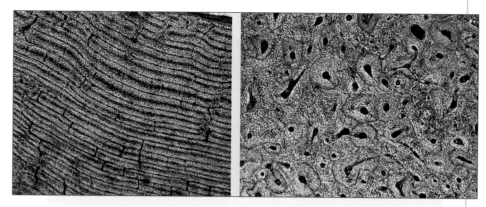

FIGURE 7.3   Photomicrograph of goat bone *(left)* and human bone *(right)* at 50× magnification. Notice the difference between the plexiform bone (goat) and the osteon (human).

remains was a tremendous challenge to the recovery effort and the identification process. Due to the extreme forces inflicted on the bodies, fragmentation was extensive in most cases. There were also non-human remains (from restaurants) and building debris that mimicked the appearance of human bone. Since forensic anthropologists are experts at working with fragmentary human remains, anthropologists became critical members in the World Trade Center recovery and identification process.

PERSONAL ACCOUNT

Amy Zelson Mundorff was the forensic anthropologist for the City of New York at the time of the World Trade Center disaster and was a responder on the scene prior to the collapse of the buildings. Her account of the work that ensued highlights the challenges presented by such a large-scale event

World Trade Center Attack

Watching the second tower collapse, I realized that there would likely be no survivors. However, what I did not grasp

was the degree to which the victims' bodies would be pulver-
ized. I also did not understand that my office would assume
the lead in conducting identifications and that I would be
assigned such a prominent role in the process. One month
into the recovery and identification process, over 6,500 pieces
of human remains had been excavated from Ground Zero. By
New Years Eve 2001, that number had doubled to over 12,000
fragments of human remains recovered and catalogued for
identification. Ultimately, approximately 20,000 fragments
of human remains were recovered from Ground Zero during
the eight months of continuous excavation (Figure 7.4).

As the only anthropologist for the City of New York, I
found myself taking on increasing responsibilities in the
identification process. The seemingly endless days blended
together in a tapestry of trauma and pain, camaraderie and
support. Although I was assigned a lead role, this was by no
means a solo effort. During that time, over 30 anthropologists from all over the United States and abroad came to assist
on rotations lasting two weeks to one year, at the site, the
landfill, and the mortuary. Our office was also flooded with
dedicated professionals from the fields of law enforcement,
forensic medicine, computer sciences and technology, and a
myriad of other fields. Looking back on the process now, I feel
that each one was absolutely critical to our eventual success.

Because of the anthropologists' particular skills in
skeletal biology, we assumed primary responsibility for
assessing which part of the body the fragments had come
from, which elements of the body were present, and if there
were any unique features to assist in identification. Had
the bodies been more intact, anthropologists would have
likely played a smaller role, but because of the severe fragmentation and decomposition, expertise in skeletal morphology became crucial. We also assumed a primary role

FIGURE 7.4 Workers examine commingled and burned bone recovered from the World Trade Center.

in re-inventorying the fragments throughout the process and in conducting a final examination to verify the accuracy of our identifications before remains were released to family members. Nearly four years later, I feel a huge sense of accomplishment for having been part of the team that worked to return the victims from the World Trade Center disaster to their families. We worked tirelessly with compassion and sensitivity. To date 10,778 of the fragments have been identified, comprising 1,597 of the 2,749 victims who died that day.

Amy Zelson Mundorff, 2005

CALCULATING THE NUMBER OF INDIVIDUALS

One of the critical questions that should be asked in situations of commingling is how many people are represented by the remains? Based on the preservation of the remains, there are various options for addressing this question. By far the most extensively utilized technique by anthropologists is the minimum number of individuals (MNI). The MNI can be calculated from either fragmentary or complete bones. When using the MNI technique, the critical concern is not to count the same individual twice. It is calculated by first taking an inventory of the bones. Next, the analyst tallies the bones by type and size, and determines which element is the most frequently observed. This value becomes the MNI. Take, for example, a scenario where you have 10 left femora, 8 right femora, 14 left humeri, and 12 right humeri. The MNI value in this case would be 14 since a minimum of 14 people (represented by left arm bones) would have to be present in order to account for the observed bone counts. As the name states, the MNI represents the absolute minimum number of individuals represented by the remains. In some instances, this number may be an accurate reflection of the actual number of individuals, but in other cases, it may underestimate the true number.

Another method for calculating the number of individuals is called the **Lincoln Index (LI)**. This method is most applicable to situations in which the bones are complete and well-preserved. With the LI, long bones are first sorted into lefts and rights. The next step is to find matched pairs (i.e., right and left elements that originated from the same person). Once this task has been completed, the relationship of paired and unpaired bones can be used to derive an estimate of the total number of individuals. The LI is calculated as $L \times R/P$, where L = total number of left bones from a single element, R = total number of right bones from that element, and P = total number of pairs for that element. As an example, imagine a scenario with 20 left femora, 15 right femora, and 12 femur pairs. In this case, the LI would be $20 \times 15/12$, or 25. With this same example, the MNI would only account for 20 individuals. The benefit of the LI is that it estimates the *actual* number of individuals, as opposed to the *minimum*, and the resulting values are much more meaningful.

8

Positive Identification

In Chapter 4, a case was noted in which a skeletonized individual was found in an abandoned building in the Bronx, New York. Using techniques previously discussed, forensic anthropological analysis indicated that it was the body of a 17- to 23-year-old black male who was approximately 73 inches (185 cm) tall. Analysis of perimortem trauma revealed two gunshot wounds to the head, indicating that his death was a homicide. A detailed review of the bones for evidence of antemortem trauma revealed healed fractures of his left tibia and fibula. There were also two metal surgical implant rods in his tibia, indicating that he had received medical attention. The healed fractures and the surgical implants were the key pieces of evidence that led to his identification. Many prosthetic devices used in surgery contain unique serial numbers that are etched into the metal along with manufacturer information. In this case, one of the rods was removed during analysis and the pertinent information was located. The company that fabricated the implants was contacted, and they were able to provide the exact date and location that the rod had been shipped. The hospital that received the shipment was contacted, and a review of their surgery logs turned up an entry detailing the treatment of a tibia fracture on a person matching the biological profile of the unidentified skeleton. Based largely on this evidence, the individual was positively identified.

In that case, as in many cases, the primary goal of forensic anthropology analysis is to achieve an identification of a missing person. It is the culmination of the various lines of evidence that narrow the field of potential candidates to a limited number of individuals. While the identification may be established strictly on the anthropological evidence, other disciplines are often instrumental in forming a **positive identification**. In order for an identification to be positive, the available evidence has to point to one person to the exclusion of all others. This is often accomplished based on a comparison of postmortem information with antemortem documentation.

COMPARISON OF DENTAL CHARACTERISTICS

One of the most accurate and efficient manners of making an identification or an exclusion with a missing person is through a comparison of dental characteristics. Specialists that work with dental identification are called forensic odontologists, or forensic dentists. While generally a forensic odontologist will formally make a dental comparison for identification, forensic anthropologists are also familiar with the human dentition, and the two disciplines work together closely. When analyzing an unidentified set of remains, it is critical that all the characteristics of the teeth are accurately documented. This is accomplished by completing a postmortem charting that records all missing, filled, and unrestored teeth in the unidentified individual's mouth. Postmortem X-rays are also taken for comparison and are of utmost importance.

Sometimes, one of the most difficult tasks in the identification process is to find antemortem X-rays and treatment records. Usually it is the role of law enforcement personnel to track down these records through interviews with friends and relatives. Even if a missing person's dentist can be located, this does not guarantee that the records have been archived and retained. Assuming that antemortem radiographs do exist, the antemortem/postmortem comparison is generally very straightforward, especially if there has been a large amount of restorative work. No two fillings are the same, so comparing dental radiographs is similar to fingerprint comparison and a match between the two establishes a positive identification.

X-RAY IDENTIFICATION

Besides dental radiographs, almost any antemortem X-ray of the skeleton can be potentially used to make an identification. Some more common types of antemortem X-rays include those of the head and chest. Radiographs of the head in the anterior-posterior plane will likely reveal outlines of the frontal sinuses. These are air pockets located in the forehead just above the eyes. In X-ray, they are very distinctive and are cauliflower-shaped in appearance. Studies have shown that no two frontal sinuses share the same pattern, and comparison with the head X-rays of an unidentified person can provide conclusive evidence for an identification. Similarly, there are many skeletal features contained within a chest X-ray due to the quantity of ribs and vertebrae. These can also be quite useful for identification purposes, especially if there was any type of surgical procedure.

The type of radiographic evidence described above was a crucial component in the resolution of a mystery that had its origins dating back to the Vietnam War. In 1967, a single-seat RF-101C aircraft collided with a UH-1B helicopter. Although the

RF-101C pilot survived, everyone on the helicopter was killed. The helicopter was known to be carrying U.S. personnel, but the identity of one individual on the aircraft went unsolved for almost 34 years. Due to relentless investigative work, a potential match to a missing U.S. civilian contractor was eventually discovered. There were no antemortem dental records available and the only available antemortem radiographs consisted of a chest X-ray. Comparison of the size and shape of the clavicle in the antemortem chest X-ray with a clavicle recovered from the helicopter crash site in Vietnam assisted in the man's identification. Based in part on this evidence, the remains were identified in May 2001 as Jerry Degnan, and his remains were returned to his brother for burial.[23]

FACIAL RECONSTRUCTIONS

When all other lines of evidence fail, it is possible to make facial reconstructions based on the features of the skull. Some forensic anthropologists specialize in this skill that brings together art and science. In the traditional approach, markers are placed throughout the cranium and mandible as a guide to re-create the soft tissue depth. Clay is then placed over the bone using the markers as guides and the face is modeled. Unless some amount of hair and soft tissue was present with the body, many of the key features that would make a person visually recognizable are left to the skill of the artist. For example, hair style, lip thickness, ear shape, and nose dimensions may be very subjective. Besides the clay reconstructions, some scientists will work on the computer or with pencil drawings. Recently, the skulls from several unidentified individuals from New York City have been taken to the New Jersey State Police Laboratory in Hamilton, New Jersey, in order to complete composite sketch reconstructions (pencil drawings) in collaboration with scientists and law enforcement personnel. A sketch artist first draws an exact replica of the skull. Then, with the help of forensic anthropologists, tissue thickness and features are added to the skull. The benefit of this type of reconstruction is that they can be completed within a couple hours and they look very lifelike (Figure 8.1). The resulting sketch can then be distributed in flyers or published in newspapers in an effort to help identify the person. These types of reconstructions alone cannot make a positive identification, but they can be instrumental in drawing attention to the case with the goal that someone will see the image and recognize similarities with a missing person. Once a potential lead is received, more conclusive lines of evidence (e.g., dental records) will have to be used to make the identification positive.

DNA IDENTIFICATION

DNA analysis is a recent scientific advance that has made it possible to positively identify previously unidentifiable sets of remains. This technique is used to distinguish between individuals using only samples of their DNA (deoxyribonucleic acid), the molecule that encodes genetic information. Since DNA can be extracted from bones and teeth, this type of forensic analysis is very useful in many forensic anthropology cases. It is of particular utility if the bones are very fragmentary, which precludes the use of other means of identification. A prime example of the important role of DNA involves the effort to identify the victims from the World Trade Center attack, most of which have been identified through DNA comparison. DNA analysis is still expensive and time-consuming, but when all other means of identification fail, it is often the method that can supply a name to an unknown person. Due to the increased accessibility to DNA and its prominence in forensic casework, at least a general understanding of DNA analysis is in the best interest of forensic anthropologists. Along these lines,

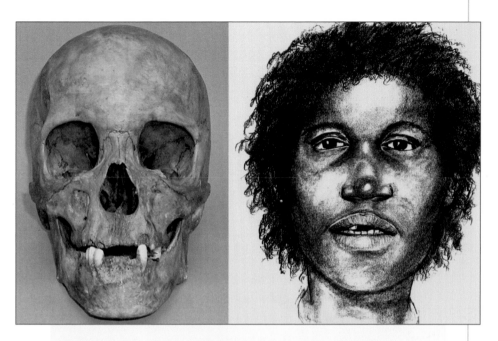

FIGURE 8.1 Cranium of an unidentified black female and a composite sketch created based on her skeletal and dental features.

those studying forensic anthropology should take courses relating to molecular biology if possible. Although certainly not necessary in all cases, the power of DNA in the identification process cannot be overstated.

Overall, each case presents its own unique set of challenges, and all available antemortem and postmortem evidence must be considered in order to determine if a positive identification is possible. Ideally, fingerprints, dental X-rays, or some type of antemortem information will be available to make the identification rapid, straightforward, and conclusive. If not, less traditional means, such as facial reconstructions, may have to be employed in order to try and find a potential match. Finally, if traditional identification methods such as fingerprint or dental analysis are not possible, DNA analysis is an excellent means of identification.

9 Conclusion

After the analysis is completed and all of the anthropological findings are compiled, the final step in the process is the filing of a case report. A forensic anthropology case report should briefly detail the background of the case, including details of any recovery efforts; provide a summary of the analytical findings; and then describe exactly how the determinations of age, race/ancestry, sex, stature, trauma, and time since death were made. It is important to remember these reports are legal documents and may be viewed by attorneys, family members, investigators, and others. As such, the report can be introduced into evidence and used in legal proceedings. Furthermore, the author of the report may be called as an expert witness to testify. All statements in the report must be defensible in a court of law and they should be presented in a manner that is intelligible to a judge and jury. The report is the culmination of all of the forensic anthropologist's work and, thus, should be concise yet detailed. It is quite likely that opposing attorneys will have outside experts scrutinize the report for inconsistencies. The implications of this report may be considerable, especially in criminal proceedings.

It is hoped that after reading this book, you will have gained an appreciation of the role of a forensic anthropologist in medicolegal investigations. Most forensic anthropologists have experience founded in the fields of anthropology, archaeology, and human osteology. Application of these specialized skills can help unlock vital clues in both the outdoor and laboratory settings. Generally, forensic anthropologists work on badly decomposed or skeletonized bodies that are not candidates for routine autopsy, but this is not always the case. In most instances, the goal of the analysis is to reconstruct the biological profile of the decedent and include documentation of all antemortem and perimortem trauma. While it would be nearly impossible to detail all of the possible scenarios faced by practicing forensic anthropologists, this book has made an attempt to use several real-life case examples to highlight some of the most common applications of the discipline. One final note, contrary to what might be portrayed in popular whodunit television programs, the resolution of a medicolegal case relies on a vast array of forensic scientists and diverse types of analyses. Furthermore, this work may take weeks or months to fully research and synthesize. Comprehensive and definitive answers are seldom instantaneous. Although integral in many situations, it is important to remember that forensic anthropology is just one piece in the investigative puzzle.

NOTES

1. K.S. Field, *History of the American Academy of Forensic Sciences: 50 Years of Progress 1948–1998.* Published for the American Academy of Forensic Sciences (West Conshohocken, Pa.: American Society for Testing and Materials, 1998).

2. D.D. Thompson, "Forensic Anthropology," in *A History of American Physical Anthropology, 1930–1980,* ed. F. Spencer (New York: Academic Press, 1982), pp. 357–369.

3. D.H. Ubelaker, "J. Lawrence Angel and the development of forensic anthropology in the United States," in *A Life in Science: Papers in Honor of J. Lawrence Angel,* ed. J.E. Buikstra (Kampsville, Ill.: Center for American Archeology, 1990), pp. 191–200.

4. H.H. Mincer, E.F. Harris, and H.E. Berryman, "The A.B.F.O. study of third molar development and its use as an estimator of chronological age," [published erratum appears in *J Forensic Sci* 38(6) (1993):1524] J Forensic Sci 38(2) (1993): 379–390.

5. T. McKern and T. Stewart, *Skeletal Age Changes in Young American Males.* Technical Report EP-45 (Natick, Mass.: Headquarters Quartermaster Research and Development Command, 1957).

6. C.L. Brace, "Region does not mean 'race'—reality versus convention in forensic anthropology," *J Forensic Sci* 40(2) (1995): 171–175.

7. N.J. Sauer, "Forensic anthropology and the concept of race: if races don't exist, why are forensic anthropologists so good at identifying them?" *Soc Sci Med* 34(2) (1992):107–111.

8. S. Rhine, "Non-metric skull racing," in *Skeletal Attribution of Race, Methods for Forensic Anthropology,* eds. G.W. Gill and S. Rhine (Albuquerque, N.Mex.: Maxwell Museum of Anthropology, 1990), pp. 9–20.

9. M.J. Hinkes, "Shovel shaped incisors in human identification," in *Skeletal Attribution of Race, Methods for Forensic Anthropology,* eds. G.W. Gill and S. Rhine (Albuquerque, N.Mex.: Maxwell Museum of Anthropology, 1990), pp. 21–26.

10. L.W. Konigsberg, N.P. Herrmann, and D.J. Wescott, "Commentary on: McBride DG, Dietz MJ, Vennemeyer MT, Meadors SA, Benfer RA, Furbee L. 'Bootstrap methods for sex determination from the os coxae using the ID3 algorithm,' *J Forensic Sci* 2001;46:424-428." *J Forensic Sci* 47(2) (2002): 424–427.

11. T.W. Phenice, "A newly developed visual method of sexing the os pubis," *Am J Phys Anthropol* 30(2) (1969): 297–301.

12. W.M. Bass, *Human Osteology,* 5th ed. (Columbia, Mo.: Missouri Archaeological Society, 2005).

13. P. Willey and T. Falsetti, "Inaccuracy of height information on driver's licenses," *J Forensic Sci* 36(3) (1991): 813–819.

14. M. Trotter and G.C. Gleser, "Estimation of stature from long bones of American whites and Negroes," *Am J Phys Anthropol* 10 (1952): 463–514.

15. M. Trotter and G.C. Gleser, "A re-evaluation of estimation of stature based on measurements of stature taken during life and of long bones after death," *Am J Phys Anthropol* 16 (1958): 79–123.

16. D.H. Ubelaker and B.J. Adams, "Differentiation of perimortem and postmortem trauma using taphonomic indicators," *J Forensic Sci* 40(3) (1995): 509–512.

17. H.E. Berryman and W.M. Gunther, "Keyhole defect production in tubular bone," *J Forensic Sci* 45(2) (2000):483–487.

18. W.M. Bass, "Outdoor decomposition rates in Tennessee," in *Forensic Taphonomy: The Postmortem Fate of Human Remains*, eds. W.D. Haglund and M.H. Sorg (Boca Raton, Fla.: CRC Press, 1997), pp. 181–186.

19. W.D. Haglund, "Dogs and coyotes: postmortem involvement with human remains," in *Forensic Taphonomy: The Postmortem Fate of Human Remains*, eds. W.D. Haglund and M.H. Sorg (Boca Raton, Fla.: CRC Press, 1997), pp. 367–381.

20. W.D. Haglund, D.T. Reay, and D.R. Swindler, "Canid scavenging/disarticulation sequence of human remains in the Pacific Northwest," *J Forensic Sci* 34(3) (1989): 587–606.

21. W.R. Maples and M. Browning, *Dead Men Do Tell Tales* (New York: Doubleday, 1994).

22. A.Z. Mundorff, "Urban anthropology: Case studies from the New York City Medical Examiner's Office," in *Hard Evidence: Case Studies in Forensic Anthropology*, ed. D.W. Steadman (Upper Saddle River, N.J.: Prentice Hall, 2003), pp. 52–62.

23. B.J. Adams and R.C. Maves, "Radiographic identification using the clavicle of an individual missing from the Vietnam conflict," *J Forensic Sci* 47(2) (2002): 369–373.

GLOSSARY

Anatomical position Standardized orientation for a person's body. The individual is situated in a standing or laying position with his or her arms at his or her sides and palms facing forward.

Antemortem Before death.

Anterior The front part of a bone when the body is in anatomical position.

Articulation The union of two skeletal elements along a joint or suture. For example, the femur articulates with the tibia at the knee joint.

Biological profile A person's demographic information, including his or her age, sex, height, and ancestry.

Caucasoid A term used to describe a person's race or ancestry; used synonymously with white and European.

Cause of death Usually the disease or injury responsible for initiating a lethal sequence of events. An example would be a gunshot wound of the head or atherosclerotic cardiovascular disease (heart attack).

Commingling The intermixing of body parts from two or more individuals. For example, if the bones of several people were jumbled together, they would be referred to as commingled.

Compaction Density. When describing soil, compaction is an indication of the firmness or looseness of the dirt. Differences in soil compaction may be an indication of a hidden grave.

Craniometric data Measurements taken between specific landmarks on the skull.

Cranium The skull without the lower jaw.

Deciduous When describing teeth, this refers to the baby, or milk, teeth.

Diaphysis The shaft of a bone.

Distal The part of the bone that is farthest from the head when the body is in anatomical position. Most frequently used to describe portions of long bones.

DNA analysis A technique used to distinguish between individuals using only samples of their DNA (deoxyribonucleic acid), the molecule that encodes genetic information in cells.

Epiphyses (sing., epiphysis) The ends, or caps, of a bone.

Forensic anthropology The application of physical anthropology and archaeology to medicolegal matters. Forensic anthropologists are experts on the human skeleton and use bones to interpret age, sex, height, ancestry, and trauma. They are also commonly involved in the recovery of human remains from various types of scenes.

Forensic entomology The study of insects in the medicolegal context.

Forensic odontologist Dentist that specializes in working with cases in the medicolegal realm, most often related to the identification of individuals based on a comparison of their dental records.

Forensic stature Self-reported height, such as might be found on a driver's license.

Forensic taphonomy The study of what happens to a body from the time of death until the time of discovery. This might include decompositional changes or animal scavenging of the remains.

Gracile Small or delicate. This term is used to describe morphological size.

Human osteology The study of the human skeleton.

Inferior The lowermost portion of a bone, generally used in reference to the cranium.

Kerf The walls and floor of a cut caused by a knife or saw in bone. Characteristics of the kerf can be important for determining specific information about the tool.

Lateral The part of a bone that is farthest from midline when the body is in anatomical position.

Law of superposition States that as layers of soil accumulate, the deeper layers (and the items associated with these layers) are older than the ones encountered above them.

Lincoln Index (LI) A technique that is used to quantify the number of individuals represented by a group of commingled bones. In most cases, it provides a more accurate estimate than the minimum number of individuals (MNI).

Manner of death   Categorization of death based on the evidence and the circumstances surrounding a person's death; usually classified as natural, accident, homicide, suicide, or undetermined.

Measured stature   Precise documentation of living height, such as might be found in military or medical records.

Medial   The part of a bone that is closest to midline when the body is in anatomical position.

Medicolegal   Relating to medicine and the law. Often this implies an investigation into unexplained, unexpected, or violent deaths.

Minimum number of individuals (MNI)   A technique that is used to quantify the number of individuals represented by a group of commingled bones.

Mongoloid   A term used to describe a person's race or ancestry; used synonymously with Native American and Asian.

Negroid   A term used to describe a person's race or ancestry; used synonymously with black or African.

Perimortem   Occurring at or around the time of death.

Physical anthropology   A branch of anthropology that deals with evolution and human variation; forensic anthropology is an applied application within this field.

Plan map   A sketch map that shows the location of important features and artifacts in two dimensions. It depicts a horizontal section of the site (e.g., ground surface), as though the observer was above the area looking down upon it.

Positive identification   The identification of a person to the exclusion of all other possible candidates, often achieved through dental records, fingerprints, medical records, or DNA analysis.

Postcranial skeleton   The bones located below the head.

Posterior   The back part of a bone when the body is in anatomical position.

Postmortem   After death.

Profile map   A sketch map that shows the location of important features and artifacts in two dimensions. It usually depicts a vertical section of the site after excavation (e.g., ground surface to 1 meter deep), as though a slice was made through the area and the observer was looking at it from the side.

Proximal   The uppermost portion of a bone; the part that is closest to the head when the body is in anatomical position.

Pubic symphyses (sing., symphysis)   A specific area of the pelvis located in the front of the body; important for determining the age at death of adults.

Robust   Large or pronounced. This term is used to describe morphological size.

Strata (sing., stratum)   A layer of soil that can be differentiated from other layers based on color, texture, compaction, and so on.

Stratigraphy   Analysis of soil layers.

Subadults   Anyone that has not reached adulthood, including infants, children, and adolescents.

Superior   The uppermost portion of a bone, generally used in reference to the cranium.

Sutures   Zigzagging, immobile joints that join the various bones of the cranium together.

BIBLIOGRAPHY

Adams, B.J., and L.W. Konigsberg. "Estimation of the most likely number of individuals from commingled human skeletal remains." *Am J Phys Anthropol* 125 (2004): 138–151.

Adams, B.J., and R.C. Maves. "Radiographic identification using the clavicle of an individual missing from the Vietnam conflict." *J Forensic Sci* 47 (2002): 369–373.

Bass, B., and J. Jefferson. *Death's Acre*. New York: G.P. Putnam's Sons, 2003.

Bass, W.M. "The occurrence of Japanese trophy skulls in the United States." *J Forensic Sci* 28 (1983): 800–803.

Bass, W.M. "Time interval since death: A difficult decision." In *Human Identification: Case Studies in Forensic Anthropology*, edited by T.A. Rathbun and J.E. Buikstra. Springfield, Ill.: Charles C. Thomas, 1984.

Bass, W.M. "Outdoor decomposition rates in Tennessee." In *Forensic Taphonomy: The Postmortem Fate of Human Remains*, edited by W.D. Haglund and M.H. Sorg, 181–186. New York: CRC Press, 1997.

Bass, W.M. *Human Osteology*. 5th ed. Columbia, Mo.: Missouri Archaeological Society, 2005.

Berryman, H.E., and W. M. Gunther. "Keyhole defect production in tubular bone." *J Forensic Sci* 45 (2000): 483–487.

Brace, C.L. "Region does not mean 'race'—reality versus convention in forensic anthropology." *J Forensic Sci* 40 (1995): 171–175.

Brooks, S., and J.M. Suchey. "Skeletal age determination based on the os pubis: a comparison of the Acsádi-Nemeskéri and Suchey-Brooks methods." *Human Evolution* 5 (2005): 227–238.

Byrd, J.H., and J.L. Castner, eds. *Forensic Entomology: The Use of Arthropods in Legal Investigations*. Boca Raton, Fla.: CRC Press, 2001.

DiMaio, D.J., and V.J.M. DiMaio. *Forensic Pathology*. 2nd ed. Boca Raton, Fla.: CRC Press, 2001.

Field, K.S. *History of the American Academy of Forensic Sciences: 50 Years of Progress 1948–1998*. Published for the American Academy of Forensic Sciences. West Conshohocken, Pa.: American Society for Testing and Materials, 1998.

Gruelich, W.W., and S.I. Pyle. *Radiographic Atlas of Skeletal Development of the Hand and Wrist*. Palo Alto, Calif.: Stanford University Press, 1959.

Haglund, W.D. "Dogs and coyotes: postmortem involvement with human remains." In *Forensic Taphonomy: The Postmortem Fate of Human Remains*, edited by W.D. Haglund and M.H. Sorg, 367–381. Boca Raton, Fla.: CRC Press, 1997.

Haglund, W.D., D.T. Reay, and D.R. Swindler. "Canid scavenging/disarticulation sequence of human remains in the Pacific Northwest." *J Forensic Sci* 34 (1989): 587–606.

Hinkes, M.J. "Shovel shaped incisors in human identification." In *Skeletal Attribution of Race, Methods for Forensic Anthropology*, edited by G. W. Gill and S. Rhine, 21–26. Anthropological Papers Vol. 4. Albuquerque, N.Mex.: Maxwell Museum of Anthropology, 1990.

Iscan, M.Y. "Wilton Marion Krogman, Ph.D. (1903–1987): The end of an era." *J Forensic Sci* 33 (1988): 1473–1476.

Iscan, M.Y., S.R. Loth, and R.K. Wright. "Age estimation from the rib by phase analysis: White females." *J Forensic Sci* 30 (1985): 853–863.

Iscan, M.Y., S.R. Loth, and R.K. Wright. "Metamorphosis at the sternal rib end: A new method to estimate age at death in white males." *Am J Phys Anthropol* 65 (1984): 147–156.

Maples, W.R., and M. Browning. *Dead Men Do Tell Tales*. New York: Doubleday, 1994.

Marks, M. K. "William M. Bass and the development of forensic anthropology in Tennessee." *J Forensic Sci* 40 (1995): 741–750.

McKern, T., and T. Stewart. *Skeletal Age Changes in Young American Males*. Technical Report EP-45. Natick, Mass.: Headquarters Quartermaster Research and Development Command, 1957.

Mincer, H.H., E.F. Harris, and H.E. Berryman. "The A.B.F.O. study of third molar development and its use as an estimator of chronological age." [published erratum appears in *J Forensic Sci* 38(6) (1993): 1524.] *J Forensic Sci* 38 (1993): 379–390.

Mulhern, D.M., and D.H. Ubelaker. "Differences in osteon banding between human and nonhuman bone." *J Forensic Sci* 46 (2001): 220–222.

Bibliography

Mundorff, A.Z. "Urban anthropology: Case studies from the New York City Medical Examiner's Office." In *Hard Evidence: Case Studies in Forensic Anthropology*, edited by D.W. Steadman, 52–62. Upper Saddle River, N.J.: Prentice Hall, 2003.

Ousley, S., and R. Jantz. *FORDISC 2.0*. Knoxville: University of Tennessee, 1996.

Ousley, S.D. "Should we estimate biological or forensic stature?" *J Forensic Sci* 40 (1995): 768–773.

Phenice, T.W. "A newly developed visual method of sexing the os pubis." *Am J Phys Anthropol* 30 (1969): 297–301.

Sauer, N.J. "Forensic anthropology and the concept of race: if races don't exist, why are forensic anthropologists so good at identifying them?" *Soc Sci Med* 34 (1992): 107–111.

Scheuer, L., and S. Black. *Developmental Juvenile Osteology*. San Diego: Academic Press, 2000.

Sledzik, P.S., and S. Ousley. "Analysis of six Vietnamese trophy skulls." *J Forensic Sci* 36 (1991): 520–530.

Stewart, T. *Essentials of Forensic Anthropology*. Springfield, Ill.: Charles C. Thomas, 1979.

Symes, S.A., H.E. Berryman, and O.C. Smith. "Saw marks in bone: Introduction and examination of residual kerf contour." In *Forensic Osteology*, edited by K. J. Reichs. 2nd ed. Springfield, Ill.: Charles C. Thomas, 1998.

Symes, S.A., J.A. Williams, E.A. Murray, J.M. Hoffman, T.D. Holland, J.M. Saul, et al. "Taphonomic context of sharp-force trauma in suspected cases of human mutilation and dismemberment." In *Advances in Forensic Taphonomy*, edited by W.D. Haglund and M.H. Sorg, 403–434. Boca Raton, Fla.: CRC Press, 2002.

Thompson, D.D. "Forensic Anthropology." In *A History of American Physical Anthropology, 1930–1980*, edited by F. Spencer, 357–369. New York: Academic Press, 1982.

Todd, T.W. "Age changes in the pubic bone I: The male white pubis." *Am J Phys Anthropol* 3 (1991): 285–334.

Trotter, M., and G.C. Gleser. "Estimation of stature from long bones of American whites and Negroes." *Am J Phys Anthropol* 10 (1952): 463–514.

Trotter, M., and G.C. Gleser. "A re-evaluation of estimation of stature based on measurements of stature taken during life and of long bones after death." *Am J Phys Anthropol* 16 (1958): 79–123.

Ubelaker, D.H. "The forensic anthropology legacy of T. Dale Stewart (1901–1997)." *J Forensic Sci* 45 (2000): 245–252.

Ubelaker, D.H. "J. Lawrence Angel and the development of forensic anthropology in the United States." In *A Life in Science: Papers in Honor of J. Lawrence Angel*, edited by J.E. Buikstra, 191–200. Kampsville, Ill.: Center for American Archeology, 1990.

Ubelaker, D.H., and B.J. Adams. "Differentiation of perimortem and postmortem trauma using taphonomic indicators." *J Forensic Sci* 40 (1995): 509–512.

Willey, P., and T. Falsetti. "Inaccuracy of height information on driver's licenses." *J Forensic Sci* 36 (1991): 813–819.

FURTHER READING

Most forensic anthropology books that are geared toward the general public (i.e., not scientific publications) are compilations of interesting case examples. The following are some of the most popular titles and represent a well-rounded account of the types of cases a forensic anthropologist might encounter.

Bass, W.M., and J. Jefferson. *Death's Acre*: *Inside the Legendary Forensic Lab the Body Farm Where the Dead Do Tell Tales*. New York: G.P. Putnam Sons, 2003.

Koff, C. *The Bone Woman: A Forensic Anthropologist's Search for Truth in the Mass Graves of Rwanda, Bosnia, Croatia, and Kosovo*. New York: Random House, 2004.

Maples, W. R., and M. Browning. *Dead Men Do Tell Tales: The Strange and Fascinating Cases of a Forensic Anthropologist*. New York: Doubleday, 1994.

Steadman, D. W. (ed.) *Hard Evidence: Case Studies in Forensic Anthropology*. New York: Prentice Hall, 2002.

Ubelaker, D. H., and H. Scammell. *Bones: A Forensic Detective's Casebook*. New York: M. Evans and Company, Inc., 2000.

Web Sites

American Academy of Forensic Sciences

http://www.aafs.org/

The leading association of forensic specialists in the United States. One component of the organization is the branch of physical anthropology, which includes forensic anthropologists. Many of the most important research papers are published in the *Journal of Forensic Sciences*.

Argentine Forensic Anthropology Team

http://www.eaaf.org/

Homepage of the Argentine Forensic Anthropology Team, a group of forensic anthropologists working on human rights cases throughout the world. Its Web site provides a look at its mission and work.

Bone Specialist on Call

http://www.smithsonianmag.com/issues/2000/april/mall_apr00.php

In this informative article, anthropologist Michael Kernan gives a detailed account of forensic specialists identifying missing children and victims of various disasters.

C.A. Pound Human Identification Laboratory

http://web.anthro.ufl.edu/capoundlab.shtml

Web site with information about the forensic anthropology program at the University of Florida and the C.A. Pound Human Identification Laboratory.

Discovering Dominga

http://www.pbs.org/pov/pov2003/discoveringdominga/special_evidence.html

In 2001, the Guatemalan Forensic Anthropology Foundation conducted an investigation into genocide cases in Guatemala. A detailed analysis of what they discovered is provided.

ForensicAnthro.com

http://www.forensicanthro.com

This site provides information on academic programs, books, Web sites, and associations that focus on forensic anthropology.

Forensic Anthropology Center at the University of Tennessee, Knoxville

http://web.utk.edu/~anthrop/index.htm

Includes information about the graduate program, body donation for the research facility, publications available from the department, and more.

Gray's Anatomy of the Human Body

http://www.bartleby.com/107/

The entire book *Gray's Anatomy* available online. Excellent and very detailed information on skeletal anatomy and its relationship to soft tissue.

History Detectives

http://www.pbs.org/opb/historydetectives/techniques/forensic.html

This site includes a basic but thorough definition and description of forensic anthropology.

Further Reading

Joint POW/MIA Accounting Command
http://www.jpac.pacom.mil/
Provides information about the Joint POW/MIA Accounting Command and its
effort to recover and identify U.S. military personnel that are missing from past
conflicts. The Central Identification Laboratory is staffed by forensic anthropologists and is the world's largest forensic anthropology laboratory.

OsteoInteractive
http://library.med.utah.edu/kw/osteo/index2.html
This site provides a wealth of information on forensic anthropology, human
osteology, paleopathology, and histology, and includes links to books, articles,
news items, academic programs, conferences, and more.

Reading the Remains
http://www.pbs.org/wgbh/nova/icemummies/remains.html
This site provides a detailed account of anthropologists Charles Higham and Ra-
chanie Thosarat's discovery of a prehistoric grave and what they learned from
analyzing the remains found inside.

PICTURE CREDITS

figure:

1.1: Bradley J. Adams
2.1: Courtesy of EAAF
2.2: Infobase Publishing
2.3: Infobase Publishing
2.4: Infobase Publishing
3.1: Bradley J. Adams
3.2: Infobase Publishing
3.3: Courtesy JPAC
4.1: Bradley J. Adams
4.2: Bradley J. Adams
4.3: Bradley J. Adams; based on Gruelich and Pyle 1959
4.4: Bradley J. Adams; photographs by Stephanie Mittak
4.5: Bradley J. Adams; photographs by Stephanie Mittak
5.1: Infobase Publishing
6.1: Bradley J. Adams; photograph by Stephanie Mittak
6.2: Bradley J. Adams; photographs by Stephanie Mittak

6.3: Infobase Publishing
6.4: Bradley J. Adams; photographs by Stephanie Mittak
6.5: Bradley J. Adams
6.6: Courtesy of University of Tennessee, Dept of Anthropology
6.7: Courtesy of University of Tennessee, Dept of Anthropology
7.1: Bradley J. Adams; photograph by Gina Santucci
7.2: Bradley J. Adams; photographs by Stephanie Mittak
7.3: Courtesy of D. Benedix and M. Tersigni
7.4: Office of Chief Medical Examiner, New York City
8.1: Bradley J. Adams; sketch drawn by Lewis Trowbridge with assistance from Donna Fontana

Cover: Michael Donne, University of Manchester/Photo Researchers, Inc. (main); PhotoDisc (spot)

INDEX

ABOUT THE AUTHOR

Bradley J. Adams, Ph.D., is an expert in the field of forensic anthropology. He is currently the forensic anthropologist for the Office of Chief Medical Examiner (OCME) in New York City. He is also an adjunct lecturer at Hunter College and Pace University, holds a faculty position at the New York University Medical Center, and frequently lectures in the New York City area on topics relating to forensic anthropology. In his present position with the OCME, Dr. Adams is responsible for all forensic anthropology casework in the five boroughs of New York City (Manhattan, Brooklyn, Queens, the Bronx, and Staten Island). His responsibilities also include supervision and analysis of World Trade Center remains. He serves as a critical member of the OCME disaster response team.

Prior to accepting the position in New York, Dr. Adams was a forensic anthropologist and laboratory manager at the Central Identification Laboratory (CIL) in Hawaii from 1997 to 2004. While with the CIL, Dr. Adams directed large-scale recovery and investigation operations in remote locations, including Burma, Indonesia, Vietnam, Cambodia, Laos, Papua New Guinea, Kiribati, South Korea, North Korea, Nicaragua, and Panama. These operations were conducted in order to recover the remains of missing U.S. military personnel. Dr. Adams has also served as an expert witness, worked on several archaeological excavations, and has published numerous articles in peer-reviewed journals.

ABOUT THE EDITOR

Lawrence Kobilinsky, Ph.D., is a professor of biology and immunology at the City University of New York John Jay College of Criminal Justice. He currently serves as science advisor to the college's president and is also a member of the doctoral faculties of biochemistry and criminal justice of the CUNY Graduate Center. He is an advisor to forensic laboratories around the world and serves as a consultant to attorneys on major crime issues related to DNA analysis and crime scene investigation.